WHAT PEOPLE ARE SAYING ABOUT *AUTISM MATTERS*

"As CEO of a specialty investment bank that is active in the healthcare industry with specific experience in the autism and behavioral health sectors, I found Dr. Molko's multi-faceted look at the autism landscape invaluable. Her perspective is particularly insightful, as it comes through the lens of a practitioner, an entrepreneur who has founded, built, and exited a successful autism service provider company, and an advisor to institutional investors looking to deploy capital in the space. *Autism Matters* is a must read for anyone interested in investing in the autism sector. Even more broadly, every stakeholder in the space—providers, payers, regulators, and individuals impacted by autism—can benefit from reading *Autism Matters*, as Dr. Molko holds up a mirror to the industry and identifies the key challenges, trends, and opportunities that are shaping our societal response to the autism community."

ED BAGDASARIAN

CEO OF INTREPID INVESTMENT BANKERS

"In healthcare services, clinical excellence is inextricably tied to the creation of sustainable value. In the long run, a valuable healthcare services company must be one that delivers good care and outcomes.

However, building a robust understanding of the clinical dynamics of a field like autism treatment can be challenging for investors who may more naturally be attuned to operational or financial considerations.

Resources like *Autism Matters* are invaluable in bridging the gap."

KE DING

PRIVATE EQUITY INVESTOR

"*Autism Matters* is a well written, excellent display of Dr. Molko's understanding of autistic adults' daily struggles for independence. It accurately and intricately details the many layers of the current autism services industry and points out some of the flaws in the current system. Dr. Molko asks timely and critical questions which we all must face in order to ensure we, as practitioners, continue to deliver outstanding clinical services and seek to consistently attempt to improve these services. *Autism Matters* exposes issues of critical importance: the true and long-term impact of current ABA services on autistic individuals and their families. This is an outstanding read for many audiences: families affected by autism, practitioners of autism services, and investors interested in the autism space."

GARY D. WEINHOUSE, JD/MBA

MANAGING DIRECTOR OF W CAPITAL PARTNERS

"*Autism Matters* examines why we're in need of evaluating the field of autism treatment. Ronit has made it her mission to meet the unmet demands she outlines in her book. Whether it's consulting with investors to get involved or collaborating with providers to determine better outcomes, Ronit functions with the intent of improving autism services for all parties. The insights exhibited in Ronit's book will leave you with a better understanding of why autism matters."

DR. ROB DOUK
FOUNDER & CEO OF BEHAVIORAL HEALTH WORKS

"The greatest healthcare innovators I have met combine a deep passion for the care they deliver and its impact on people's lives, with the courage and business acumen to challenge the status quo and reinvent healthcare delivery. Ronit is this leader, and from the first moment I met her I could feel her passion for autism and was inspired by the impact she has made on an entire industry."

VINCE DANIELSEN
CEO OF INLIV, A CANADIAN HEALTHCARE COMPANY

"Ronit is a compassionate and talented powerhouse in the autism arena. She brings a multi-dimensional perspective to the autism challenge—as a clinician, a service provider, a business owner, a CEO, and an investment consultant.

As a parent of a child with multiple disabilities, it is crucial that her expertise be listened to and adopted to make further advances in the field."

RANDI BUSSIN
EXECUTIVE & CAREER COACH

"The autism services arena is nascent, complex, and filled with stakeholders who have potentially competing interests. The consequences of mutual understanding between investors and providers in this market has huge consequences for society—all of us. We need someone like Ronit, who has the breadth and depth of experience to define and lead the path forward. *Autism Matters* will provide useful insights for investors, providers, families, and civic leaders who want to constructively shape the autism services market."

JULI BETWEE
PIVOT POINT MANAGING PARTNER

"*Autism Matters* is powerful, insightful, and inspiring. Dr. Ronit Molko has done an eloquent job of integrating her unique scientific, clinical, and business background to create a compelling case for investing in this dynamic and growing population segment. She makes it easy to understand why anyone interested in revenue growth combined with socially responsible investing would be smart to look into this market."

BARBARA VANDEMAN
CEO OF PARTNERSHIPWORKS

AUTISM
MATTERS

AUTISM
MATTERS

RONIT MOLKO, PhD, BCBA-D

EMPOWERING INVESTORS, PROVIDERS,
AND THE AUTISM COMMUNITY TO
ADVANCE AUTISM SERVICES

ForbesBooks

Published by ForbesBooks, Charleston, South Carolina.
Member of Advantage Media Group.

ForbesBooks is a registered trademark, and the ForbesBooks colophon is a trademark of Forbes Media, LLC.

Printed in the United States of America.

10 9 8 7 6 5 4 3 2 1

ISBN: 978-1-94663-355-2
LCCN: 2018939704

Cover design by George Stevens.
Layout design by Melanie Cloth.

This publication is designed to provide accurate and authoritative information in regard to the subject matter covered. It is sold with the understanding that the publisher is not engaged in rendering legal, accounting, or other professional services. If legal advice or other expert assistance is required, the services of a competent professional person should be sought.

Advantage Media Group is proud to be a part of the Tree Neutral® program. Tree Neutral offsets the number of trees consumed in the production and printing of this book by taking proactive steps such as planting trees in direct proportion to the number of trees used to print books. To learn more about Tree Neutral, please visit **www.treeneutral.com.**

Since 1917, the Forbes mission has remained constant. Global Champions of Entrepreneurial Capitalism. ForbesBooks exists to further that aim by bringing the Stories, Passion, and Knowledge of top thought leaders to the forefront. ForbesBooks brings you The Best in Business. To be considered for publication, please visit **www.forbesbooks.com.**

For my mother, whose shining light went out before her time. Witnessing her struggle and experiencing her loss set me on a path of reflection and inquiry. It is with her memory and beautiful spirit in my heart that I discovered my purpose: to empower others.

And for all those who have the power to lift others up: may this book demonstrate the profound impact you can truly make.

TABLE OF CONTENTS

INSPIRED ACTION

FOREWORD

Until the mid-1960s, there were no demonstrably effective interventions, training, or educational approaches for children or adults with autism. As noted in *Autism Matters*, this changed thanks to pioneering research at the University of Washington, University of Kansas, and UCLA. A host of serious behavioral challenges were shown to be able to change for the better and, of most importance, systematic approaches taught language to children with autism who lacked language skills. Parents and educators saw hope and progress that had never been previously experienced. Yet, these approaches were not panaceas, as many children did not progress as well as others and many children showed behavior changes only in the settings in which they received intervention. Improvements occurred as parent training became a major theme. Like many advances in medicine, education, and other areas of behavioral sciences, the field somewhat struggled, as it lacked systems for implementation, policies, funding other than small research trials, recognition of social/ecological factors that affected implementation, and certification of providers or training programs. As these areas started being addressed, and as the growth of the number of providers and funding sources developed, policy changes allowed and mandated insurance coverage for autism services. Thus, behavioral health companies and investors began acquiring companies providing autism services.

Prior to *Autism Matters*, there had been no comprehensive source for investors, parents, clinicians, providers, communities, or policy-makers. Here, in everyday language, is the first book that offers an opportunity for the variety of consumers it serves to learn state-of-the-art information about autism and provides an astute review of current interventions that allows the reader to be able to recognize what is successful, what needs improvement, and what to look for to avoid making serious mistakes in choosing one service over another. Be it parents in desperate need of finding a program that will teach language to their child, an investment group buying a program that offers a fiscally sound investment and addresses all ethical issues in serving families and their children, or policy makers creating informed judgments about laws and regulations to ensure safe, effective service delivery in autism services, *Autism Matters* is an invaluable resource. This book will also be very useful for the bur-geoning expansion of start-up autism service companies in that they will have a resource that will help them avoid pitfalls that most new companies face.

Autism Matters is remarkably easy to read and even has a touch of dry humor, giving it the sense of realism that is often missing in so many resource books. There is deep coverage of applied behavior analysis (ABA) which is, by far, the most common kind of approach offered by companies in the field. Throughout *Autism Matters,* the reader is helped to understand how to look for and decide which ABA services fit their family or agency and investors learn which kinds of ABA would be the best fit for the kind of investment they want to make.

In my career of nearly fifty years in which I have been deeply involved in ABA and was, for some time, president of my own company offering ABA services, I cannot think of anyone with a better background than Dr. Molko to have authored this outstanding book. She has impressive academic credentials and background, has published research, has owned one of the largest and best autism services programs, and has wisely interviewed people with autism, parents, providers, stakeholders, and investors before writing this book. She is a savvy businesswoman and a humanist who can relate to the complicated issues facing the consumers of this book and their concerns. *Autism Matters* will become a seminal reference for all of its potential readers and will be cited and valued for many years to come.

John R. Lutzker, PhD
Distinguished University Professor
School of Public Health
Georgia State University
Past President of the American Psychological Association
Division for Intellectual and Developmental Disabilities/
Autism Spectrum Disorder

ACKNOWLEDGMENTS

The idea to write a book is an easy one. Actually executing the idea and bringing it to fruition is an immense amount of work. This book is the brainchild of two seemingly casual conversations which unexpectedly led me down a path of deep and often uncomfortable exploration. It would not have been possible without the invaluable contributions of many incredibly supportive and generous individuals, including:

My husband, my hero, Daryn, for his unwavering support, love, and commitment to us, our family, and our life together. You took on so many daily family and parenting responsibilities so that I could work on this project for hours into the night.

My children, Elan and Kayden, for your immense amount of patience, humor, and understanding, and for the sacrifices you made so I could take the time to get this done. You are my greatest gifts.

My father, for working so hard to get us out of South Africa, and my brother, for joining us in California to keep our family geographically adjacent. My life would have been very different without the study and career opportunities afforded to me in the U.S.

Chris McGoff, who launched me on this book writing journey and spent countless hours sharing his wisdom and encouraging me to "just get it done." From you I have learned about culture by design, the power of vulnerability, and how business transformation can initiate personal transformation.

All the team members at Advantage Media who helped me immeasurably. Special thanks and appreciation to Keith Farrell, my writing partner, who immersed himself in a crash course in everything autism and patiently worked with me through multiple re-writes to get everything exactly how it needed to be. My deepest gratitude to Eland Mann and Lauren Franceschini, my editorial team, for working tirelessly to refine the message of this book. And the rest of the team, including Kirby Andersen, Justin Batt, Laura Otero, Ben Coppel, Deborah Ridgill, George Stevens, Patti Boysen, Katherine Beck, Carly Blake, Melanie Cloth, Carson Russell, and others who not only worked so hard to bring this project to completion, but also embraced me as an Advantage|ForbesBooks family member.

There are many individuals who shared their stories, views, and experiences with the understanding that they remain anonymous, either because they do not share their autism diagnosis publicly, or for other reasons. To those autistic individuals, parents, stakeholders, state and government employees, bankers, investors, and professionals, I am deeply grateful for your time, your transparency, and your willingness to contribute to this important message.

John Lutzker, for believing in me from the day we met, my third day living in the United States, and for guiding me professionally and personally ever since. You taught me about ethical and evidence-based practice and you and Sandra have shown me what love for family and true partnership looks like; you are the epitome of an honorable man.

Gary Weinhouse, for demonstrating true collaboration through the toughest of times and the moments of triumph. Thank you for your support, commitment, and friendship.

Ed Bagdasarian and Adam Abramowitz, for guiding me through one of the most challenging and rewarding experiences of my career and for continuing to support me on my path.

And finally, to those individuals who read early drafts and provided invaluable feedback, who provided hours of conversation and insight for this project, and who assisted me on this journey, including Evian Gordon, Ke Ding, C. Russell Bryan, Rob Douk, Vince Danielsen, John Rogers, Kristin Jacobson, Judy Mark, Karen Báez, Sara Gershfeld Litvak, KC Baker, Mari-Anne Kehler, and my fellow ASLA board members.

RONIT M. MOLKO, PhD, BCBA-D

CEO & PRINCIPAL, EMPOWERING SYNERGY

Ronit Molko is a dynamic senior executive and entrepreneur recognized for combining strategic vision and technical expertise to drive business initiatives. In 2001, Dr. Molko cofounded Autism Spectrum Therapies Inc. (AST), which grew into a highly respected, multi-state provider of services for individuals on the autism spectrum. In 2014, she sold her company to Learn It Systems, a private-equity-backed strategic buyer, and served as President of Autism Services for the combined family of companies until early 2016.

Today, as CEO and Principal of Empowering Synergy, Dr. Molko consults as an expert in the field of service delivery for healthcare, with a special focus on behavioral healthcare and companies that provide services to families affected by autism and developmental disabilities. Drawing on her unique background, which includes both business and clinical expertise, she conducts due diligence for investors looking to make a difference by investing in the behavioral healthcare industry and helps clients think strategically about expansion, develop high-value business relationships, and better articulate their vision, mission, strategy, and corporate culture.

During her time as CEO of AST, Dr. Molko launched and grew the company into an operation that employed over seven hundred people and provided long-term, sustainable solutions that improved daily life for clients and their families across multiple states. Under her leadership, AST continually met the increasing demand for scale and growth while retaining the integrity of its mission, vision, and culture. Dr. Molko forged strong working relationships with both regulators and third-party payers, preserving services for her clients throughout regulatory changes. She also drove strategies to diversify revenue streams, increase profitability, and improve efficiency while providing consistently excellent programs and client service. Dr. Molko fostered a continuous learning culture, providing extensive training to develop talent in professionals and management while advancing AST's entrepreneurial approach. The company has been recognized by community and government entities as a market leader that provided cutting-edge, highly relevant programs.

Dr. Molko is currently a board member of the Galt Foundation and the Los Angeles Chapter of the Autism Society of America. She is also a member of the Women Presidents' Organization. Throughout her career, Dr. Molko has been actively involved in many healthcare-based committees and organizations.

In recognition of her business prowess and leadership abilities, Dr. Molko has received many awards, including the Mickey Weiss Award for Outstanding Alumni from the American Jewish University, the World of Difference 100 Award in Education from The International Alliance for Women, an Enterprising Women of the Year Award from *Enterprising Women* magazine and the Smart Leader

Award from Orange County's Smart Leaders. She was recently named as one of L.A. Biz's Women of Influence honorees for 2017.

Dr. Molko completed Harvard Business School's three-year Owner/President Management program. Prior to that, she earned a PhD in Applied Behavioral Science and Family Life from the University of Kansas, a master's degree in Psychology from Claremont Graduate University and a BA in Psychology from the American Jewish University. She completed a post-doctoral fellowship at the UCLA Department of Psychiatry and Biobehavioral Sciences. Dr. Molko is a licensed clinical psychologist in California and Washington states, and became a board-certified behavior analyst in 1999.

FOR PROVIDERS AND INVESTORS

MEETING OF THE MINDS

A year prior to writing this book, I was sitting in my office when the phone rang. I answered, and a deep male voice said, "Hello, I'm looking for a girlfriend."

My initial reaction was that this must be a prank call, and I should hang up. Curiosity got the better of me, however, so I asked where he had gotten my number. He told me he'd found it on LinkedIn. I was skeptical, but as he continued to talk, it made sense why he was reaching out to me.

Not long after that call, I received another communication on LinkedIn, an email that read: "Can you help me find a friend? I have not hung out with a friend in a year. I want someone to go to McDonald's with and have a burger."

These two young men who reached out to me for support were autistic. They found me because of the work I have done with autistic children and families and believed I might be able to help them. Their doing so, and the conversations that followed, sparked a year-long quest for me to interview as many individuals with autism and their families as I could. I also set out to speak with stakeholders in the autism services industry: service providers, state and federal funding agencies, insurance companies, and legislators.

My goal was to assess how we, as a service industry and as a society, are setting up autistic children to be self-reliant adults living fulfilled and independent lives. What I discovered is that overall, the system is failing them.

And what's more, the voice of these individuals with autism is a powerful and growing one. It is creating the next wave of demand for services that are going to completely reshape how we think about, invest in, and regard services for individuals with autism in our country.

MY BACKGROUND IN AUTISM SERVICES

For nearly three decades, I have worked in the field of autism services in several roles, including licensed clinical psychologist, entrepreneur, CEO, and corporate behavioral healthcare consultant. My work with some of the leading figures in autism intervention[1] facilitated my extensive background in autism research, family systems, and clinical services. I also launched my own autism services company from my dining room table, which I helped grow to become one of the

---

1 An intervention is any kind of treatment, therapy, activity, or the provision of a service that is designed to improve the functioning and quality of life for individuals. There are many types of interventions for autism aimed at different aspects of functioning such as communication, social interaction, and patterns of behavior. Some of these interventions have substantial scientific evidence to support their efficacy, others have limited evidence, and some have none.

largest providers in California—as well as a national success—and later sold to a private-equity-backed strategic investor. I am in the unique position of understanding the scientific, clinical, and business applications of autism intervention and, having served as a CEO of my autism services company and as a consultant conducting due diligence for investors across the nation, I am able to see the autism services landscape from the perspective of both the provider and the investor.

What I have seen is that, when properly empowered, individuals, organizations, and communities can make a positive, sustainable impact. The autism services provider market is dedicated to making such impacts for individuals, and I have witnessed how simple shifts have profoundly affected people and expanded their horizons and opportunities. Together with investors, autism services can affect not only individuals and their families, but also entire communities. A positive intervention outcome translates to a better quality of life for both the individual and their loved ones. I have written this book to inform investors about autism, the services provider market, and the investment opportunities in this industry to illuminate what I believe are the important issues that need to be understood and addressed. Ultimately, my goal is to advance outcomes for autistic individuals, inform society about why we should value and celebrate neurodiversity, and give investors a guide to making a positive impact and strong returns.

This book examines what the autism services industry looks like today and why investment in this market is beneficial for both providers and consumers of the services. While it is primarily aimed at investors and examining the investment opportunity the field of autism services presents, it also speaks to providers, the need to progress the industry, and how private equity investors can help do so. It also takes a critical look at the industry and asks, "How have we done? Where have we fallen short? How do we evolve autism services? How do we do better?" The objective is to start a conversation about where the industry is headed, what its larger objectives should be, and why change is necessary. Each area of discussion presents opportunities for conscious investors who want to see their capital make a positive impact on the world. Together, investors and providers can succeed and empower the autistic community.

In addition to the book's primary target audience, I have taken steps to ensure that the autism community's voice is represented as well. After all, it is their welfare and well-being that ultimately drive us. With that consideration, it is important to note that this book uses both person-first language and condition-first language. There are strong opinions on both sides regarding how to refer to individuals who are living with autism. The scientific and professional communities tend to use person-first language ("individual with autism"); however, many autistic adults prefer condition-first language ("autistic individual"). Some feel it is important to emphasize the individual, not the condition, whereas many self-advocates say being autistic is a part of who they are and that referring to them as "a person with autism" denies their identity. I can appreciate and respect both opinions on this matter, and as such, the book uses both terminologies.

MEETING OF THE MINDS

How would you define a good quality of life? For many, it means having a productive job that provides for their needs, independence, strong personal relationships, and success in accomplishing their goals. Put simply, we want to be able to decide where we live, what we do, and with whom we spend our time.

Does this differ for individuals who experience challenges with physical or developmental disabilities? It should not be surprising to learn that such individuals generally want the same things as everyone else: independence, employment, pursuit of their passions, and meaningful relationships. Individuals on the autism spectrum want to have control over their own lives and make decisions about where they live, with whom they live, and how they spend their time.

The focus of my work has been behavior-based interventions grounded in the principles of applied behavior analysis (ABA), the most widely funded methodology for autism intervention today and considered by most to be the gold standard for the industry. ABA is the science in which strategies and procedures derived from the principles of behavior are systematically applied to effect changes in socially significant behaviors. I will discuss ABA in more detail later on in this book to provide context for why it has become the intervention of choice for most funding sources and families. I will also analyze the complexities around this service delivery model in the current market of autism services.

I cofounded a behavioral service provider company that became one of the largest autism service providers in the nation. After selling our company in 2014 and receiving calls from individuals and families asking questions much like the previously discussed messages from those two young men, I found myself outside of the provider market looking in and wondering, "How have we done?" In response, I have dedicated the recent past to interviewing as many people in different arenas of the autism services industry as I could, gaining perspective on how we, as an ABA provider group, are meeting the needs of our clients.

As part of this journey, I returned to the annual Autism Society National Conference, where I met with and learned about the personal journeys of many self-advocates and parents of children on the spectrum. Many adults with autism refer to themselves as *self-advocates*. Self-advocacy in the autistic community has a specific and important significance for the adults who have taken over the responsibility of their well-being. They are able to effectively communicate with others and, in turn, receive the support they need and want.

Autism-Society.org defines self-advocacy as "knowing when and how to approach others to negotiate desired goals, build better mutual understanding and trust, and achieve fulfillment and productivity," and notes that "successful self-advocacy often involves an amount of disclosure about oneself to reach the goal of better mutual understanding."

The annual Autism Society National Conference provides a platform for self-advocates to participate in panel discussions and symposia on various topics relevant to living with autism. I listened as they were each asked what they considered to be a good quality of life. One by one, they gave answers that were typical of most people. Listening to them reinforced my perspective that most autism intervention programs are shortsighted. Their answers were relatable and, in many ways, predictable. Yet, as many of them described, these goals had not been considered in their intervention programs.

Many of these self-advocates had received some ABA intervention during their childhood and teenage years, which helped them learn to communicate and better interact with their environments. The methodology has decades of research to support its efficacy at bringing about meaningful improvement in quality of life and acquisition of skills in individuals with autism and other disorders. However, after years spent providing ABA services, I was shocked to discover that many ABA recipients experienced serious issues and deficits in adulthood. ABA services in the current autism industry are insufficient to equip autistic individuals with the skills required to live as independently as possible. Listening to individuals who have experienced ABA emphasizes just how true this is.

It is striking to me that these long-term quality of life goals are not typically factored into the services these individuals receive. The majority of funding and intervention services have been appropriately aimed at young children on the spectrum, because the earlier intervention begins, the better the long-term outcomes tend to be. And while many providers say they only work with children, the truth is that if you work with a child with autism, you are working with the adult they will become.

> *If you work with a child with autism, you are working with the adult they will become.*

Considering this, it is alarming that these programs are not viewing children as the adults they will become. The programs are often not focused on providing the children with the tools they'll need to work, live, and function in the world. That is particularly distressing considering that half a million children with autism are currently aging into adulthood without adequate skills and support.[2]

The conference showcased current issues facing families, especially as the population of autistic individuals matures. But in a way, it also demonstrated just how far the autism marketplace has evolved since I first began working in it. Not only have attitudes and perceptions changed, but we now have a community of self-advocates to

---

2   Amy Lennard Goehner, "A Generation of Autism, Coming of Age," *The New York Times*, last modified April 13, 2011, http://www.nytimes.com/ref/health/healthguide/esn-autism-reporters.html.

listen to and inform us, which is incredibly valuable. These individuals have a voice that is getting louder and shifting the demand for services. They are engaging on issues that affect them—a dramatic change from past decades.

The self-advocates at the conference spoke about their needs, what they wanted out of life, and ways in which society could better support their goals. One individual spoke at length about the importance of being in the "least restrictive environment" at school. In 1975, the Education for All Handicapped Children Act (EHA, or EAHCA) was passed, giving disabled individuals a right to public education, with specific focus on an education plan with parental input that would mirror the education of nondisabled students. The act was revised numerous times between 1975 and 2004, ultimately being renamed the Individuals with Disabilities Education Act (IDEA) and focusing more on the individual, expanding the law to cover autism (in 1990), promoting research and improved outcomes, providing for transition programs after high school and requiring that education be provided in neighborhood schools. The act also includes the right of individuals to have the least restrictive environment possible in order to support the achievement of their goals and pursuit of opportunities. The aim was to provide children with disabilities the same opportunities available to typically developing children, as opposed to automatically placing them in restrictive classroom settings with limited educational experiences, which often severely limit opportunities.

Others spoke about being accepted for who they are, as well as having their own thoughts, feelings, and dreams. I often hear self-advocates say they want to make their own choices, but that many people don't allow them to. The system has been set up in a way that often renders self-advocates powerless by denying them the opportunity to make their own decisions, even though they have the right to do so. It's why you'll see people at conferences wearing badges that read, "Nothing about me without me," a slogan borrowed from political movements and disability activism campaigns of the 1990s.[3] They're tired of people making decisions about them without their own voices directing their future.

The reason why decisions are made for them, without their consent, is due to a general and long-standing stigma that individuals with autism must battle. "I have to work much harder than anyone else to get what I want or even to be heard," is something many autistic individuals have told me. They have to work harder to prove themselves at school or at work because of the many misperceptions people have about autism. Rather than taking the effort to learn about them, their talents, and their challenges, people often see autistic individuals as incapable, unintelligent, and/or peculiar.

Many of the conference speakers expressed their wish that people would take more time to understand them instead of trying to change who they are. They share a common desire to be accepted and to not be pressured or forced to be "typical," or different than they are. This extends to school, work, and personal relationships. Like you and I, individuals with autism need personal relationships; they want to experience personal intimacy. Forging such relationships can be very difficult for autistic individuals, as understanding and expressing emotions is challenging.

The conference was incredibly insightful and strongly reinforced what my inquiry over the past year had demonstrated. While we have come far in terms of understanding autism and helping those who live with it, the journey I took to write this book also emphasized

---

3   James I. Charlton, *Nothing About Us Without Us: Disability Oppression and Empowerment* (California: University of California Press, 2000).

how far we have yet to go. More so than in years past, it increased my awareness by highlighting the needs of adults and the amount of work still to be done in helping young children gain the skills they need to survive outside of their home environments.

THE NEEDS OF A GROWING MARKET

When we launched our company, the delivery and implementation of ABA were evolving. Service providers were moving ABA from clinic and research environments to more natural environments, such as clients' homes and schools, to meet the demand for services. Additionally, research suggested that providing intervention in the actual settings that children needed to learn how to navigate would enhance their generalization (the ability to apply learned skills to different situations) of the skills they were learning. That change in approach to treatment, along with the rapidly growing demand for services, led to the autism services industry we have today, where providers teach skills using ABA techniques and strategies, as well as other interventions, in autistic individuals' communities and homes.

As the industry has grown, there has been an increase in prevalence and diagnosis. When I first entered the field, 4.5 of every 10,000 children were being diagnosed with autism. Today, that number has radically increased to 1 in 59[4]—a global phenomenon of rapidly increasing diagnosis rates. It is suspected that a significant proportion of that increase derives from better diagnostic criteria. However, that does not rule out some increase in incidence.

---

4   Catherine Rice, "Prevalence of Autism Spectrum Disorders --- Autism and Developmental Disabilities Monitoring Network, Six Sites, United States, 2000," *Morbidity and Mortality Weekly Report 56*, no. SS01 (February 2007): 1-11; Jon Baio, et al., "Prevalence of Autism Spectrum Disorder Among Children Aged 8 Years —Autism and Developmental Disabilities Monitoring Network, 11 Sites, United States, 2014," Surveillance Summaries 67, no. 6 (April 27, 2018): 1-23, http://dx.doi.org/10.15585/mmwr.ss6706a1.

Regardless of why the numbers are increasing, the spike in diagnoses has spurred a rapidly growing services industry, which is now intensely attracting investors. In many ways, this is a positive development, which will result in increased funding, more access, and better services for those who need them. However, there are caveats to consider.

ABA service providers have yet to establish agreed-upon standards of measurement when it comes to determining the outcomes of intervention. ABA is the process, not the outcome: the change in behavior or the acquisition of skills is the measured outcome. While the science provides for methodologies to examine outcomes in ABA, the atmosphere in the service provider market has generally been one of competition and not one of cooperation; providers measure their individual outcomes and protect their proprietary data. Such is the nature of business. Despite the recent efforts of some providers and researchers to establish collaborative sharing of outcome measurements, minimal progress has been made. Unfortunately, because of the unique composition and purpose of the autism services industry, this lack of cooperation is proving detrimental to progress both for the clients and for the industry as a whole.

The lack of established standards in autism services has created a vacuum, which third-party payers—those who typically pay for the services—are beginning to fill. Put simply, absent clear and definable standards and outcome measures as an industry, insurance companies are beginning to dictate what services should be provided, what they should look like, and how outcomes should be measured, ultimately determining future funding opportunities. As insurance companies in general have a limited appreciation for the complexity and nuances of a good ABA program, this issue is becoming quite problematic.

Later in this book, I will go into further detail about how insurance companies are taking the wheel when it comes to autism services and how it is hurting the provision of those services. To be sure, both increased insurance coverage of autism services and an increased interest from private equity are good for the industry. We have to ensure that it is industry experts—and not individuals with far less, if any, expertise within an insurance company—deciding how best to provide services and measure outcomes. Along these same lines, professionals within our industry must ensure that private equity is invested in the right places to advance best practices and ensure good outcomes along with the return on investment that they seek.

We are approaching a critical period in autism services. With a growing population of maturing and aging individuals living in the community without the ability to care for themselves, service providers must start looking further into the future. How can we better provide long-term outcomes that enable a real quality of life? What is the next evolution of the implementation of ABA?

Gaining a new perspective through my interviews with stakeholders and evaluations of ABA service providers and companies has helped bring some important things into focus. My unique experience and viewpoints have also allowed me to offer my services as a consultant, conducting due diligence for investors, helping them evaluate acquisition targets, and helping providers improve their operations and grow their services. I have seen the challenges and successes of many different types of providers of autism services and within behavioral healthcare.

By viewing the autism services industry from different angles, I have been able to gain perspective on where we must focus our attention. The long-term quality of life outcomes that have such an impact on an individual's adult life are not sufficiently emphasized. We are failing to provide the skills necessary for lifetime fulfillment through independent living, employment, and the formation of interpersonal relationships. This is, without a doubt, a shortfall of current autism intervention services.

AUTISM SERVICES: THEN AND NOW

When I entered the field in the late 1980s, there weren't many self-advocates we could engage with and learn from. At that time, the autistic adult population was mostly comprised of severely affected individuals living at home, in group homes, or in institutions. They were deemed incompatible with the general community. They had mostly not had the benefit of intensive, early intervention and were not exposed to a life involving choice and self-advocacy. Young children were often not being identified and diagnosed, and most were not receiving the kinds of services that are currently available.

Today we are able to talk to many autistic individuals who have received intervention, and we can assess how they've benefited and what they still need. Most autistic individuals today are not living in institutions and, thanks to legislation like IDEA, children are no longer deprived of basic rights and access to educational services simply because they are considered disabled. The progress has been wonderful, satisfying, and rewarding.

The conversation has shifted, as well. Twenty-five years ago, the conversation among clinicians and service providers was geared toward "fixing" autistic individuals and making them appear as typical or "normal" as possible. Now, with input and pressure from self-advocates and their families, who have lived this journey alongside them, that conversation has evolved. These days, the focus is on helping individuals with autism understand and interact with their environments and communicate more effectively. There is a growing awareness today that autistic individuals don't need to be fixed or cured—they need to be understood, included, accommodated, accepted, and appreciated.

As these understandings have grown, that knowledge has affected intervention programs. When I first entered the field, the majority of clinical programs were rote, rigid, and impersonal. Today, intervention has evolved, and many programs are taking a more individualized, naturalistic approach focusing on each individual's interests and strengths. Many different programs have been developed using ABA methodology as intervention and have moved beyond the clinic setting and into schools and homes. That has spurred the growth of an entire service delivery industry. However, as we will discuss later in the book, while that growth has increased access, it has also diluted the quality and integrity of the implementation of ABA in the field.

Proper support and understanding goes a long way toward making a difference in the lives of individuals with autism. While the autism services industry has improved greatly over the past few decades, the industry still has more to learn about the experience of being autistic. As we grow to understand autism more, we can help services providers and the general public to better understand and accept autism.

Many adults with autism do not receive a diagnosis until well into adulthood. I spoke to a woman who, like many adults, did not discover she was on the autism spectrum until she was fifty. Prior to that, she couldn't understand why she had been unable to forge long-standing relationships with others and struggled in her work environment. Once she discovered she had autism, her entire life changed. She was able to access support groups and make friends.

She met a man who is also on the spectrum and is now her husband. Having an understanding of who she is and how her mind works has opened up a whole new world for her.

Many adults describe how receiving a diagnosis helped them put the puzzle pieces together and make sense of their lives. Ethan Cross, an international best-selling and award-winning author of eight novels, describes how finally receiving his diagnosis explained so much about his life and his interactions with the world. His preference for being alone and the social anxiety he experienced in groups had governed some of his life decisions, and now this made sense to him. Ethan describes his struggles with anxiety and depression and how challenging and exhausting it is to live, work, and socialize in what feels like an "alien" world.[5] Every adult I interviewed shared similar experiences and struggles with anxiety and depression.

The aim of the autism services industry is to help more individuals live fully satisfying and rewarding lives, something many adults have figured out how to do by choosing careers and living environments that support their needs and challenges and allow them to express their gifts and strengths. Individuals with autism don't need to be fixed—they need help relating to and engaging with their surroundings, communicating, and understanding social cues. They also need support in finding work opportunities, understanding how their environments can help or hinder them, and learning what modifications can improve these environments. Today, clinicians and service providers understand these needs much better than we did when I first began working in the field. However, the conversation must continue to evolve.

---

5   Ethan Cross, "How getting an autism diagnosis as an adult changed me," Autism Speaks, last modified November 16, 2016, https://www.autismspeaks.org/blog/2016/11/16/how-getting-autism-diagnosis-adult-changed-me.

My doctoral studies were fulfilled in a new and unique joint doctoral program created by my undergraduate advisor, Dr. John Lutzker, in Los Angeles and Dr. James Sherman at the University of Kansas. As the University of Kansas was the one of the headquarters of the creation of ABA, I not only had the privilege of studying with some of the greatest minds in ABA, I also gained fundamental, hands-on ABA experience and witnessed the incredible power of ABA when applied with proper ethics, morals, and good intentions. I worked in a center-based ABA program where we conducted early intervention and research on the efficacy of the programs and in an in-home program working with families living in rural areas. It was here that I first experienced the potential impact of ABA on extreme self-injurious and harmful behaviors, and the improvement in quality of life. Studying in Kansas, where some of the forefathers of ABA were rooted, was an extremely formative experience that provided an invaluable foundation for my professional career. To learn more about the work I did in Kansas as well as the power of ABA, please refer to the further reading and information section.

Upon completion of my coursework in Kansas, and while conducting my dissertation research in child maltreatment, I was presented with an opportunity that led me down the path to intensive in-home ABA services. Dr. John Lutzker owned a company that provided services, including a day program, to adults with developmental disabilities. He wanted to begin an in-home behavioral treatment program for children with autism, which I helped him launch and manage in Los Angeles. This is where I gained my initial experience running the operations side of a company that provides services to individuals with developmental disabilities, including managing and supervising the staff, developing clinical programs, managing service delivery, and collaborating with funding sources. After graduating with my doctorate, I went to UCLA to complete my post-doctorate.

During my post-doctorate fellowship in developmental disabilities at UCLA, I spent a year in the department of psychiatry and biobehavioral sciences. My time was divided between the Neuropsychiatric Institute, the UCLA Autism Evaluation Clinic, and Lanterman Developmental Center (LDC), an institutional setting promoting progressive habilitation training for individuals with developmental disabilities.

LDC was one of the California "state hospitals" originally designed in the 1920s to house individuals with developmental disabilities for life. Here I worked with individuals with megalencephaly (a condition in which an infant or child has an abnormally large brain size, resulting in seizures, partial paralysis, and cognitive impairment) and children who were medically fragile, requiring specialized, twenty-four-hour care. I worked with individuals with autism as well as individuals with psychiatric diagnoses. Part of the work I performed was conducting comprehensive assessments to examine the needs of adults who had been living at LDC since childhood and were now being transitioned into community based housing.

Following an initiative to transition almost all individuals with developmental disabilities into community settings, LDC transitioned its last resident back into the community in December 2014, and, along with many other institutions in California over the past years, was closed.

At UCLA, I worked at the Neuropsychiatric Institute which included an inpatient residential treatment program, an outpatient day program for children with autism, and outpatient services for children with a broad range of behavioral, developmental, and psychiatric disorders.

My most relevant work was in the Autism Evaluation Clinic learning about the assessment and diagnosis of autism. This year spent in autism diagnostics was a critical time. The word "epidemic" began to be associated with autism in 2000, and the Autism Diagnostic Observation Schedule (ADOS) was published that same year and became commercially available a year later. This was a significant development in the quality of the comprehensive nature of diagnostic tools available for assessing autism and other PDDs.

. . . .

THE HUMAN ELEMENT

Another area that has been brought into sharper focus as I consider the industry is the need to emphasize the individual receiving care. It's too easy to focus solely on the diagnosis or the science and lose sight of the human being.

I first saw this in practice while I was completing my undergraduate studies under the supervision of my professor and advisor, Dr. John Lutzker, at a facility where I worked directly with patients with traumatic brain injuries to address their behavioral challenges. The staff were having a myriad of issues with behavioral outbursts, and they asked us to conduct assessments and devise behavior support plans. It was in this capacity that I worked with the individual who gave me my first experience with a recurring problem in intervention programs and care models for individuals with neurodevelopmental issues.

He was a former stunt man who had been injured at work after an accident during which he dove into a shallow pool. He suffered a debilitating brain injury, which resulted in paralysis, blindness, some communication deficits, and having to live his life in a care facility.

As a behavior specialist, I was tasked with conducting a functional behavior assessment to determine why he was screaming and displaying aggression every morning when his care provider would wake and shower him. To assess the situation, I observed his morning routine and noticed something that should have been fairly obvious.

This man was blind, and his care provider was not informing him of what was happening each morning. Imagine being blind and lying in bed, sleeping, and then being woken up, moved to a wheelchair, and bathed without any communication of what is occurring. It is understandable that this gentleman would scream; he had no warning and little engagement from staff to help him prepare for what his routine would be. Additionally, they would sometimes put him into the chair in the shower without first warming the water.

My behavior plan was relatively simple. Along with creating a schedule he could understand and teaching the staff the basics about antecedents, behavior, and consequences, a large part of my work with this individual was teaching the staff to simply talk to him, to communicate the daily routine, and to make sure the shower was warm before they put him in. The facility was impressed by the rapid reduction in his behavioral outbursts. For our team, the solution was obvious: be compassionate, and treat him like a human being.

The staff were treating him like a task, not a person. He was just another number they had to get out of bed and shower—another check mark on their list of responsibilities. The human consideration was almost completely missing. There was a lot of dehumanizing behavior in institutions and residential settings at the time, and sadly, I have heard numerous stories from self-advocates about feeling the same way in their ABA therapy. Clinicians and caregivers can get too focused on methodology or getting through a program, sometimes forgetting that there is a person behind the diagnosis with whom they need to connect on a personal level.

It's important that we as autism services providers, researchers, clinicians, caregivers, and business leaders don't lose sight of the human element. We must continue to deliver care and provide services, but in a humane way that preserves autonomy and dignity and respects the individuality, emotions, and experiences of the individuals we serve.

LOOKING AHEAD

I left the Autism Society Conference enthusiastic about how far we have come over the past decades in terms of understanding and aiding individuals with autism. Though we are growing in our understanding, my experiences also reaffirmed the needs of adults with autism and highlighted the deficits that currently exist in the provider community. While positive impacts have been made, it is unacceptable that a growing segment of our population must accept the status quo. There is still significant room for improvement.

The more time I spent talking with people connected to all aspects of the autism community, the more determined I became to find ways to progress the industry and elevate its outcomes. In the time that I have been working in the field, I have seen continued advancement. But in most professional circles, what I hear is that people think we've found the magic and universal "answer" in our current delivery and implementation of ABA. While ABA is a remarkable methodology based on decades of science that has had an outstanding impact on many lives, many of the current service delivery models are neglecting the critically important long-term functional outcomes and ignoring that the beneficiaries of these interventions are ill-prepared to live, work, and relate to their fullest potential as adults.

I've written this book to spark questions: What comes next? How do we improve upon existing models? What should outcomes look like, and what should the provider market and investors in that market be thinking about? What do self-advocates tell us they need? What has the current implementation of ABA failed to give them?

These self-advocates and their families are a vital resource. They allow us to gauge how well we are doing as service providers. By listening to them and their families, we can get an accurate picture of the experience of receiving services, what autism services do well, and what needs improvement. By utilizing the feedback and input of people who have grown up with ABA, we can build and improve upon it.

While ABA service models have given critical skills to individuals and benefited them in many ways, there are many areas where long-term quality of life is not being achieved. There is a large, aging population of autistic adults who do not live on their own and instead reside with their parents or a relative. When these individuals' parents or relatives pass on, what will happen to them? Who will care for them? Many of them are unable to find work or hold jobs, even though they want to. Consider that hundreds of thousands of autistic teens will become adults in the next decade. These individuals need to be properly supported as self-advocates.

Whether we are autistic or neurotypical,[6] we all want the same basic things from life. Almost everyone defines a good quality of life in the same terms: productiveness, independence, and loving rela-

---

6   Neurotypicals, or NTs, are individuals not characterized by neurological patterns of thought and behavior that are considered to be atypical, such as autism or other neurological disorders. Autistic individuals refer to individuals without autism, who are intellectually, cognitively and developmental typical, as neurotypicals.

tionships. We do a disservice to autistic individuals if we don't teach them the skills they need to achieve the life they want and contribute to society in return.

We can teach children with autism a myriad of skills that enable individuals to manage basic day-to-day skills such as how to tie their shoes, differentiate colors, make requests, and label objects. These are valuable skills. But many programs stop there. We need to do more. We now have a population of self-advocates telling us what they need that they didn't get, as well as many years of data showing us how we have performed in the long run as an industry. It's up to us to take that information and innovate new opportunities and programs.

In this book, we will explore what we know about autism today, current interventions and understanding why behavioral interventions are so prevalent, the current state of the autism services industry, and the outcomes of interventions. I examine where ABA is working and where gaps exist that need to be addressed. I make the case that the autism services industry needs to evolve and innovate beyond the current service delivery model and implementation of ABA, and I detail how providers and investors can best help do this. While there have been multiple recent investments and acquisitions in the autism service provider market, there is still the opportunity for a true market leader who innovates service delivery, creates stable employment for professionals, influences public policy, and focuses on meaningful long-term outcomes for individuals. My hope is that this book will encourage investment in autism services and serve as a conversation starter, inviting others from the clinical, service, and investment fields to come together and help forge new programs and opportunities that will equip autistic individuals with the skills they need to build quality, self-determined, independent lives.

CHAPTER 1

A CURRENT UNDERSTANDING OF AUTISM

Imagine your brain functioned differently than it does now. Imagine that you were just as intelligent as you are now but lacked the ability to functionally communicate with others—that your needs, wants, and preferences were difficult or even impossible to express. Think about what it must be like trying to relate to others, even just having a simple conversation, yet being unable to, because your brain doesn't easily process conversational cues like tone of voice or facial expressions. Imagine having a hypersensitivity to certain stimuli—the humming of fluorescent lights or an air conditioner—to the point where it causes you physical distress or pain yet being unable to communicate to others that stress or pain or how it limits your ability to function well in

TOPICS AHEAD:

DIAGNOSIS AND PREVALENCE

HOW AUTISM PRESENTS ITSELF

HOW ABA PROGRAMS BREAK THROUGH THE COMMUNICATION BARRIER

REFRAMING HOW WE LOOK AT AUTISM

those environments. Envision what it would be like to be incredibly intelligent and high-achieving but to avoid receiving an education because the anxiety of navigating crowds, the rules, social aspects, and interpersonal relationships of school is too overwhelming.

While it may be challenging to imagine limitations like sensory sensitivity and social or communicative challenges, autistic individuals live with a version of this reality every day of their lives.

Autism, or autism spectrum disorder (ASD), refers to a range of conditions characterized by biologically based behavioral excesses and deficits. These challenges occur in the areas of speech and nonverbal communication, social skills, and repetitive behaviors, as well as by unique talents, strengths, and differences. We now know that there is not one type of autism, but many types that fall along a spectrum, potentially caused by different combinations of genetic and environmental influences. The term "spectrum" reflects the wide variation in challenges and strengths possessed by each person with autism. The condition varies in severity and manifestation, making scientific investigation of the disorder very complex.

Most autistic individuals will stress to you that while the scientific and professional communities view autism as a spectrum, autism is not a linear condition, but rather a diverse and large number of traits that are experienced uniquely by each person. The labeling of the two ends of the spectrum as "high-functioning" versus "low-functioning" is misleading. High-functioning individuals often explain how the deficits that affect their ability to function at their highest level are typically ignored, while low-functioning individuals typically have education and program plans that focus on improving their deficits but ignore their strengths. Each autistic person will have their own set of traits and be affected by different circumstances and events.

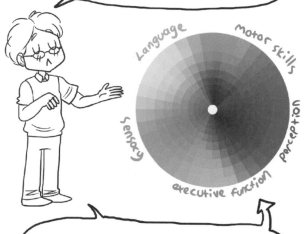

Illustrated by Rebecca Burgess

The clinical understanding of what autism is and how to help those who live with it has greatly advanced in recent years. In past decades, scientists and clinicians greatly misunderstood the disorder, which often led to individuals with autism being subjected to aversive therapies and placed in environments that were detrimental to their condition and livelihood. With advancements in the treatment options for autism, we now know that the behavioral excesses and deficits experienced by an autistic individual are amenable to change through carefully orchestrated and constructive interactions with the environment.[7]

While there are currently specific criteria for diagnosis, as outlined in the *Diagnostic and Statistical Manual of Mental Disorders*[8] (*DSM-5*), the current examination of all the possible traits that comprise autism make it almost impossible to state unequivocally that a person with autism must have a specific characteristic or trait, or that a specific trait or characteristic precludes a diagnosis of autism. As I discovered in my many interviews for this book with autistic adults, understanding and classifying autism continues to be very intricate and very personal. Having said that, the diagnostic criteria outlined by the *DSM-5* are the current scientific guidelines for diagnosing autism, which is required for eligibility to receive available and potential funding and services.

Despite popular misconceptions, autism is not the same as intellectual disability. While some individuals on the autism spectrum are cognitively and intellectually impaired, many possess average intelligence or superior intellectual abilities and extraordinary skills.

---

7   Gina Green, "Behavior Analytic Instruction for Learners with Autism: Advances in Stimulus Control Technology," *Focus on Autism and Other Developmental Disabilities* 16, no. 2 (May 1, 2001): 72-85, doi:10.1177/108835760101600203.

8   American Psychiatric Association, *Diagnostic and Statistical Manual of Mental Disorders, 5th Edition* (Arlington: American Psychiatric Publishing, 2013).

Assessing IQ in individuals with autism is tricky, as these scores may not be accurate reflections of their intellectual potential. Many children with autism lack the verbal and motor skills required to respond to the nature of the questions on IQ tests. These tests often reveal where these children are experiencing difficulty in understanding communication rather than measuring their true cognitive abilities. In previous decades many, if not most, individuals with autism were treated as if they were intellectually impaired.

Thankfully, those of us working in the field of autism today have a much clearer, science-based understanding of autism. We know it's about understanding brain function and breaking communication barriers, and we understand that individuals on the spectrum are not "broken" but rather perceive the environment differently as a result of different perceptions and brain processing. These individuals do not need to be "cured"; they need to be taught methods of communication to help them meet their needs. Additionally, they require functional, day-to-day skills that will serve them as adults living in their chosen communities and help them manage what society will demand of them. It is with these aims in mind that clinicians can help people with autism live fuller, more rewarding, and more productive lives.

My introduction to working with children with autism was during my undergraduate years in Los Angeles. I had just immigrated to the United States from South Africa for a year of study at university abroad. I enrolled in college two days after arriving and was immediately introduced to a summer camp in California. I was hired as a camp counselor in a specialized program serving children and teens with learning, emotional, and developmental disabilities.

My first experience was exciting, overwhelming, and challenging. I was living in a bunk with twelve female teens with varying learning and developmental disabilities, many of whom were away from home for the first time. There were many long nights spent comforting and coaching the girls, often unable to sleep and crying or agitated, trying to adapt to this new environment. There were also incredible moments of joy and triumph as we watched these young teens have experiences they were mostly denied in their daily lives, such as swimming with peers and group karaoke night, because of the lack of community organizations within which they could experience typical childhood activities.

After working at the summer camp, I had the opportunity to become a teacher for children with special needs and special abilities in an after-school program in Encino, California. I taught these programs to children with developmental disorders and learning challenges that included autism, Tourette's syndrome, Down syndrome, ADHD, and other learning disabilities. It was here that I met a twelve-year-old girl who was severely affected by autism.

She was virtually nonverbal, and it was very challenging to engage her in learning. Having limited experience with autism and no formal training, I was not very successful in my work with her, but she piqued my interest in autism specifically. I could see she possessed intelligence and that the burden was on me to figure out how to help her navigate her world. I became fascinated with the disorder and how to break the communication barrier. She was the spark that ignited my passion for helping individuals who live with autism. This was in 1990, before autism drew the intense attention that it now receives, before Dr. Temple Grandin became the most widely recognized face of autism, and before the word *epidemic* was associated with the disorder. Since then, I have watched the industry and its approach to autism services evolve tremendously as more research, experience, and knowledge have been acquired.

Dr. Temple Grandin is an American professor of animal science at Colorado State University, a consultant to the livestock industry, an author, and an autism spokesperson. She is one of the first people to share insights about her personal experience growing up and living with autism. Dr. Grandin speaks globally about autism and "differently abled brains." The core of her message is that autistic individuals have much to offer society and that parents should focus on building up strengths and shared interests to develop skills and "stretch kids just outside of their comfort zone to help them develop."

As our understanding of the disorder grows, so does the field of autism services. There are now clear and definable ways to aid individuals with autism. With the evolution of our field, we have a variety of methods to break through that communication barrier, and we have helpful approaches to aid individuals in learning functional life skills. Just as important, we can teach these tools and techniques to parents, teachers, and caregivers, ensuring consistency in treatment and, as much as possible, in environmental factors.

Despite this progress, there remain many popular misconceptions about autism today. In this chapter, we will discuss exactly what autism is, how it is diagnosed, how it presents, the goals of therapeutic approaches, and the ways in which society views autism.

DIAGNOSIS AND PREVALENCE

When I first began working in the field of autism over twenty-five years ago, the most cited prevalence statistic for a diagnosis of autism in children was 4.5 in 10,000. About 15 to 20 in 10,000 children were diagnosed with an autism-related condition, such as pervasive developmental disorders (PDD), pervasive developmental disorder not otherwise specified (PDD-NOS), or Asperger syndrome. Today, according to the CDC, that number is 1 in 59.[9] Researchers are still trying to understand what is driving the dramatic spike in reported autism cases, but evidence shows that improved awareness and identification of the disorder and new diagnostic criteria are major factors.

Current prevalence data[10] suggest that autism affects boys with a far greater prevalence than girls. While 1 in 37 boys are diagnosed with autism, only 1 in 151 girls are. If these numbers are accurate, boys are nearly four times more likely to develop autism. However, recent evidence suggests that autism diagnoses are being missed when it comes to females. Females tend to be diagnosed when they exhibit behavioral issues and intellectual disabilities but misdiagnosed or missed entirely when they are "higher functioning." Research has led to various conclusions as to why this is occurring. Often, when boys and girls have similar autistic traits (as determined by rating scales), boys are diagnosed, and girls are not.[11] For example, a study conducted by comparing the occurrence of autism traits and autism diagnoses in fifteen thousand sets of twins showed that girls were only formally diagnosed when they demonstrated more behavioral problems, significant intellectual disabilities, or both, despite the fact that the boys and girls had comparably high levels of ASD traits.

9   Jon Baio, et al., "Prevalence of Autism Spectrum Disorder Among Children Aged 8 Years —Autism and Developmental Disabilities Monitoring Network, 11 Sites, United States, 2014," Surveillance Summaries 67, no. 6 (April 27, 2018): 1-23, http://dx.doi.org/10.15585/mmwr. ss6706a1.

10 "Data & Statistics," Centers for Disease Control and Prevention, last updated July 11, 2016, https://www.cdc.gov/ncbddd/autism/data.html.

11 K. Dworzynski et al., "How different are girls and boys above and below the diagnostic threshold for autism spectrum disorders?" Journal of the American Academy of Child and Adolescent Psychiatry 51, no. 8 (August 2012): 788-797, doi: 10.1016/j.jaac.2012.05.018.

Other researchers believe that "high-functioning" girls are camouflaging their autism due to social pressure and/or the ability to better adapt and compensate socially.[12] The results of studies suggest that girls are able to study people and their behavior and learn social rules through observation more easily than boys.[13] This enables high-functioning girls with autism to mimic others in order to mask their traits. It has long been thought that autistic girls exhibit fewer repetitive behaviors than autistic boys, a concept that is being challenged by new research demonstrating that girls do have obsessions and repetitive behaviors; they just may be generally more socially acceptable.[14]

Due to the history of identification and diagnosis of autism in males, the diagnostic criteria have been developed specifically around males and male expression of autism. Current diagnostic criteria for autism require that an individual demonstrate, from early childhood, evidence of social-communicative and social-interaction impairments, as well as restrictive interests and repetitive patterns of behavior that cause significant impairments in functioning. Studies have shown that females have more social and communication symptoms and fewer repetitive behavior symptoms and thus are often not diagnosed, because they do not meet the current criteria.[15]

---

12 Ibid.

13 Maia Szalavitz, "Autism—It's Different in Girls," Scientific American, last modified March 1, 2016, https://www.scientificamerican.com/article/autism-it-s-different-in-girls/.

14 Frazier TW, et al., "Behavioral and cognitive characteristics of females anfdmales with autism in the Simons Simplex Collection," J Am Acad Child Adolesc Psychiatry 53, no. 3 (March 2014): 329-40, https://doi.org/10.1016/j.jaac.2013.12.004; Alexandra M Head, et al., "Gender differences in emotionality and sociability in children with autism spectrum disorders," Molecular Autism 5, no. 19 (February 28, 2014), http://doi.org/10.1186/2040-2392-5-19.

15 Kaustubh Supekar and Vinod Menon, "Sex differences in structural organization of motor systems and their dissociable links with repetitive/restricted behaviors in children with autism," Molecular Autism 6, no. 50 (September 4, 2015), https://doi.org/10.1186/s13229-015-0042-z.

An evaluation of the effect of gender on the diagnostic evaluation of autism in adults showed that gender does influence the diagnostic outcome. These researchers concluded that males and females may present with different manifestations of the disorder. They also argue that females may exhibit different, as opposed to fewer, restricted interests and repetitive behaviors than males, and that sex-specific diagnostic assessment tools are warranted to accurately evaluate the disorder in each gender.[16]

Biological and neurological differences between boys and girls may also be a contributing factor to high-functioning autistic girls receiving the wrong diagnoses. Data suggest that many high-functioning females with autism are currently misdiagnosed with mental illness. For example, 23 percent of women who are diagnosed with eating disorders have ASD symptoms, as opposed to only 3 percent of the general public.[17] Autism also tends to co-occur with ADHD, leading easily distracted females to be diagnosed with ADHD instead of autism.[18] Another misdiagnosis could be obsessive compulsive disorder (OCD), as repetitive and restricted behavior associated with ASD can mimic and present like OCD.[19]

Behavioral and preliminary neuroimaging studies support the idea that autism manifests differently[20] in girls than in boys. The brains of females with autism tend to look like those of typically developing males of the same age, with reduced activity in regions

---

16 CE Wilson et al., "Does sex influence the diagnostic evaluation of autism spectrum disorder in adults?" *Autism* 20, no. 7 (October 2016): 808–819, doi: 10.1177/1362361315611381.

17 "Statistics: How Many People Have Eating Disorders?" ANRED, https://www.anred.com/stats.html.

18 "The Relationship Between ADHD and Autism," Healthline, http://www.healthline.com/health/adhd/autism-and-adhd#overview1.

19 Marina Gask, "What is it like to be a girl with autism?" *Telegraph,* last modified July 14, 2015, http://www.telegraph.co.uk/health-fitness/body/what-is-it-like-to-be-a-girl-with-autism/.

20 Maia Szalavitz, "Autism—It's Different in Girls," Scientific American, last modified March 1, 2016, https://www.scientificamerican.com/article/autism-it-s-different-in-girls/.

of the brain normally associated with socialization (compared to typically developing females of the same age). The social behavior of females on the autism spectrum often matches those of typically developing males but scores lower than the social behavior of typically developing females on measures of empathy and friendship quality. Girls tend to perform better socially than boys and thus are less perceptible diagnostically.[21] But they still miss many social cues and struggle to fit in. Autistic women in business report losing jobs more frequently. With the new *DSM-5* criteria and the elimination of Asperger syndrome as a separate category, it is concerning that it will become even more difficult for women to receive a diagnosis without greater awareness of this issue.

After conducting many interviews for this book, almost all of the women with whom I spoke strongly believe that girls and women are misdiagnosed and under-identified, because females present differently than males, and the diagnostic criteria are designed around males. Jennifer O'Toole, creator of Asperkids LLC and author of the Asperkids book series, was diagnosed with Asperger syndrome as an adult. She likens this issue of female identification in autism to heart disease, which was historically measured in both men and women by the symptoms experienced by men. Heart disease is a leading killer and causes one in three deaths a year for women; however, women were unaware of this and did not recognize when they were experiencing a heart attack because they presented with different warning symptoms than men (for example, a woman may experience a heart attack without significant chest pain). The American Heart Association launched the "go red for women" campaign to provide informa-

---

21 Dworzynski et al., "How different are girls and boys above and below the diagnostic threshold for autism spectrum disorders?" *J Am Acad Child Adolesc Psychiatry* 51, no. 8 (August 2012): 788-97.

tion and education about the differences in signs and symptoms for women, and recent research shows that women now have far greater awareness of the risks associated with female heart disease.[22]

Similarly, O'Toole and others stress that girls and women with autism display characteristics and tendencies that are misinterpreted and misidentified, often being classified as having anxiety disorders, OCD, bipolar disorder, and eating disorders, for example. While many of these symptoms and behaviors are comorbid attributes of autism, what these women stress is that the identification of autism is being missed in these individuals, and therefore the critical interventions that can aid in alleviating many of the associated challenges are not being provided.

Treating a woman's anxiety, for example, without teaching her the social skills needed to navigate her world, does not address the heart of the issue. Some of the challenges experienced by women (and men) with autism, such as having difficulty learning that others are not always being honest or difficulties in perceiving social situations, leads to women with autism experiencing abuse and being prone to sexual assault. Almost every woman I interviewed shared a story of finding herself in a compromised position, often with a traumatic outcome, because she did not understand the innuendos and implications of the invitation she had received from a man or of the social situation in which she found herself.

As O'Toole and others clearly describe, the early diagnostic criteria and characteristics of autism disorders were defined by studying boys. Consequently, and not surprisingly, more boys are going to fit the profile that has been created when we talk about autism. As O'Toole pointed out to me during our first conversation,

---

22 Judith Gould and Jacqui Ashton-Smith, "Missed diagnosis or misdiagnosis? Girls and women on the autism spectrum," *Good Autism Practice* 12, no. 1 (May 2011): 34–41.

"We 'light it up blue' for autism awareness month, but where's the pink?"

In the past few years, far more attention has been paid to diagnostic tools and the questions being asked during assessment in an attempt to understand the different manifestations of autism and accurately diagnose women and girls. With greater awareness concerning how autism manifests in females, we can expect to see changes in the commonly accepted numbers on prevalence and diagnosis. Currently, there is more research and effort being devoted to learning more about prevalence and the gender differences.

The issue of prevalence has been a passionate topic in the autism field, with much discussion and research aimed at investigating the rise in autism rates. The first attempts to understand the prevalence of autism date back to 1966, when Victor Lotter, basing his selection on twenty-four behavioral criteria, examined the entire population of 78,000 eight- to ten-year-old children in the county of Middlesex, England. He identified thirty-five autistic children, representing a prevalence rate of 4.5 per 10,000 children, with boys being more common than girls by a ratio of 2.6 to 1.[23] This became the baseline against which other measurements of prevalence were determined, even though Lotter described in his journal article the considerable definitional difficulties within which he was working to determine his criteria for inclusion. Lotter himself acknowledged that wherever he set the bar for whether a child met the diagnostic criteria for autism would affect his prevalence number of 4.5 in 10,000. Nonetheless, Lotter's study

> "We 'light it up blue' for autism awareness month, but where's the pink?"

---

23   Victor Lotter, "Epidemiology of autistic conditions in young children," *Social Psychiatry* 1, no. 3 (December 1966): 124-135.

provided the first data from a widespread exploration of the disorder and this prevalence number of 4.5 per 10,000 remained for many years.

Since then, many studies have tried to determine the "true" prevalence of autism. Throughout the years, changes in diagnostic criteria meant that the numbers changed along with them. For example, individuals who did not qualify for a diagnosis of autism in the 1980s, based on the *DSM-3* (American Psychiatric Association, 1980; 1987), may have qualified based on new diagnostic criteria in the release of the *DSM-4* (American Psychiatric Association, 1994; 2000). This changed once again when the *DSM-5* was released in 2013, changing the criteria for diagnosis and eliminating subcategories such as Asperger syndrome, PDD-NOS, and other disorders.

The Centers for Disease Control and Prevention (CDC) began tracking the prevalence of ASD in the United States in 1998. The prevalence rates doubled from 1 in 150 children in 2000-2002 to 1 in 68 in 2010-2012.[24] The word "epidemic" became readily associated with autism in the early 2000s, and while many searched for the reason for this increase, others believed that these numbers had always been the reality and that diagnoses were simply being missed before.

Recently, researchers in Denmark set about trying to get to the bottom of the increase in autism rates by studying a very large group of children. They followed nearly 678,000 children born between 1980 and 1991, tracking them until they were either diagnosed with autism or the study ended in 2011. They looked closely at specific changes that occurred after 1994, when Denmark changed its diagnosis criteria. The team was able to determine that 60 percent of

---

24 "Autism Spectrum Disorder (ASD)," Centers for Disease Control and Prevention, last modified April 26, 2018, https://www.cdc.gov/ncbddd/autism/data.html.

the spike in diagnoses could be attributed to these criteria changes and the inclusion of outpatient data.[25] The results of this study parallel the issues faced by other groups who have tried to explore this issue of the "rise of autism." With the continuous changes in diagnostic criteria, reporting practices, and the definition of autism over the years, some children who would not have qualified for a diagnosis in the 1980s would qualify using the current criteria, and conversely, some may no longer qualify.

FAQ:

IS THE INCREASE IN DIAGNOSIS DUE TO BETTER AWARENESS? IF YES, ARE MORE HIGH-FUNCTIONING INDIVIDUALS GETTING DIAGNOSED AND IF SO, ARE THEY ELIGIBLE FOR SERVICES?

The term "high-functioning autism" is applied to individuals who are not cognitively challenged and may have deficits is areas of communication, expression, and recognition of emotions and social interaction.

Research has determined that a portion of the increase in prevalence of autism is due to better identification and diagnosis. A portion of this increase is diagnosis of individuals during adulthood, including adults recognizing themselves as being on the autism spectrum. Alternatively, some adults make this discovery when one of their children receives an autism diagnosis. More adults are seeking assessment and support as a result of greater awareness.

Eligibility for services depends on whether an individual receives a diagnosis of autism, whether that diagnosis deems them eligible for services, and whether the funding source approves the proposed program and services.

---

25 SN Hansen, DE Schendel, and ET Parner, "Explaining the Increase in the Prevalence of Autism Spectrum Disorders: The Proportion Attributable to Changes in Reporting Practices," *JAMA Pediatr* 169, no. 1 (2015): 56–62, doi:10.1001/jamapediatrics.2014.1893.

WHAT CHANGED WITH DSM-5?

THE FIFTH EDITION OF THE DIAGNOSTIC AND STATISTICAL MANUAL OF MENTAL DISORDERS

In 2013, the American Psychiatric Association published the fifth edition of the *Diagnostic and Statistical Manual of Mental Disorders (DSM-5)*, which is used by mental health professionals to diagnose behavioral and mental conditions.

Under the *DSM-4* published in 1994/*DSM4-TR* (revised in 2000), separate disorders were listed as pervasive developmental disorders with the first three comprising autism spectrum disorder:

1 AUTISTIC DISORDER

2 ASPERGER'S DISORDER

3 PERVASIVE DEVELOPMENTAL DISORDER NOT OTHERWISE SPECIFIED (PDD-NOS)

4 CHILDHOOD DISINTEGRATIVE DISORDER (CDD)

CHANGES MADE IN THE NEW DSM-5

There is only one diagnostic category—autism spectrum disorder (ASD). There are no longer subdiagnoses (autistic disorder, Asperger disorder, pervasive developmental disorder not otherwise specified, childhood disintegrative disorder). Rett syndrome is a discrete neurologic disorder.

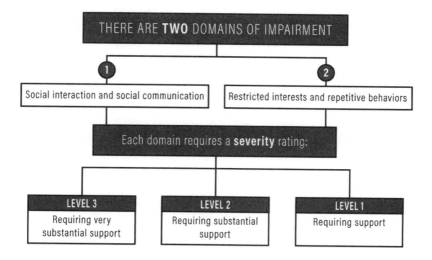

THERE ARE **TWO** DOMAINS OF IMPAIRMENT

1. Social interaction and social communication
2. Restricted interests and repetitive behaviors

Each domain requires a **severity** rating:

LEVEL 3
Requiring very substantial support

LEVEL 2
Requiring substantial support

LEVEL 1
Requiring support

An individual must display five of seven impairments

All three critieria under social interaction and social communication domain must be met. These are:

1

Problems reciprocating social or emotional interaction, including difficulty establishing or maintaining back-and-forth conversations and interactions, inability to initiate an interaction, and problems with shared attention or sharing of emotions and interests with others.

2

Severe problems maintaining relationships—ranges from lack of interest in other people to difficulties in pretend play and engaging in age-appropriate social activities, and problems adjusting to different social expectations.

3

Deficits in nonverbal communicative behaviors used for social interaction, such as abnormal eye contact, posture, facial expressions, tone of voice, deficits in understanding and the use of gestures, and a complete lack of nonverbal communication.

Two out of four criteria under the restricted interests and repetitive behaviors domain must be met. These are:

01 Stereotyped or repetitive speech, motor movements or use of objects.

02 Excessive adherence to routines, ritualized patterns of verbal or nonverbal behavior, or excessive resistance to change.

03 Highly restricted interests that are abnormal in intensity or focus.

04 Hyper- or hyporeactivity to sensory input or unusual interest in sensory aspects of the environment

Sensory differences were added to the restricted interests and repetitive behaviors domain

SOCIAL PRAGMATIC COMMUNICATION DISORDER was added to *DSM-5*. This diagnosis is given when an individual demonstrates impairment in the social communication domain but does not display restricted interests and repetitive behaviors

While more work is still needed, especially in the area of understanding how autism impacts females, we have gotten much better at identifying and diagnosing autism over the last forty years. Historically, many individuals with autism were misdiagnosed or went completely unidentified. Autistic individuals were diagnosed with all types of disorders, including childhood schizophrenia, symbiotic psychosis, disintegrative psychosis, and dementia infantilis, among others. In 2013, the American Psychiatric Association published new diagnostic guidelines for ASDs in the *DSM-5*. Previously, a person had to meet six of twelve deficits in social interaction, communication, or repetitive behaviors to be diagnosed with autism or an autism-related disorder. The new classification system eliminated the previous subcategories of autism such as Asperger syndrome, PDD-NOS, childhood disintegrative disorder, and autistic disorder and created one diagnosis of "autism spectrum disorders," and the criteria for diagnosis is much more specific.

Despite all of this, the change in definition and diagnostic criteria does not appear to account for the entire increase in autism rates. Understanding what has caused the remaining percentage of the increase is crucial to understanding factors contributing to the disorder. We can conclude that there is *some* increased incidence, even if diagnostic criteria account for a significant portion of the increase in reported cases. Some researchers believe that environmental factors—diet, pollution, certain chemicals—combined with predisposed genetic conditions trigger the development of autism, while others suggest that factors such as paternal age or the presence of certain bacteria in the mother's digestive tract during pregnancy may be causal. To this day, there is no absolute scientific consensus on what causes autism. Research suggests that multiple causes will ultimately be determined.

There is currently a lot of attention being paid to this matter. The CDC continues to devote considerable resources to tracking children on the autism spectrum over the next few years. With worldwide monitoring and a sharpened focus on autism, it is likely that scientists will soon gain a better understanding of the causes of this spectrum of disorders.

While these questions about causation are important, they can also distract from other important issues and give way to dangerous, unscientific conclusions. Many of the parents I met with believe that causal research is valuable but often consumes too much focus and resources that could be directed toward improving the lives of their children today and tomorrow by preparing them for better, more independent futures. In addition, many of these unscientific conclusions have led parents down a path to unsubstantiated and expensive "fad" treatments perpetuated by fear, stigma, and misinformation that autism is curable and should be cured. No matter what has caused the increase in reported cases, these individuals need proper and appropriate services. I do believe the increase deserves scientific inquiry; however, that is not my area of expertise nor the focal point of my work.

While these questions about causation are important, they can also distract from other important issues and give way to dangerous, unscientific conclusions.

Regardless of the reasons, the growing number of diagnoses drives home the need for higher-quality services and more consideration for the long-term needs of individuals. This is an industry that is growing in terms of both constituents requiring services and available funding avenues. Without proper resources and adequate capital, addressing any issue is impossible. Recent trends in autism should go far to encourage capital investment, which will dramatically help individuals living with autism.

HOW AUTISM PRESENTS ITSELF

Because autism falls along a spectrum, with each individual experiencing unique characteristics and challenges, it can be tricky to recognize in young children and in adults. However, people can be grouped based on similarities in behavioral and symptomatic criteria. Autism's most obvious signs tend to appear between the ages of two and three, although many parents report noticing a change or regression in their child's development as early as eighteen months. Certain developmental delays associated with autism provide subtle hints even earlier. For example, at the age when infants start to develop language—babbling and trying to communicate vocally—parents of children with autism often report that the language suddenly stops or does not develop at all. That has helped us greatly improve identification of symptoms and at-risk signs for developing autism or a developmental delay as early as six to twelve months of age.

Stephen Shore, EdD, a professor at Adelphi University and an internationally renowned expert in the study of autism, tells the story of being struck with what he refers to as the "autism bomb." As a toddler, after eighteen months of typical development, he lost functional communication, experienced behavioral meltdowns, and withdrew from the environment. He was diagnosed with autism in the early 1960s, and the doctors recommended that his parents institutionalize him. His parents refused and instead provided him with an intensive program emphasizing music, movement, sensory integration, narration, and imitation. Shore credits his parents for accepting who he was while also recognizing the gravity of the challenges he had to overcome to lead a fulfilling life. Music is a critical component of Shore's life and a communication tool for him, and he utilizes social stories to help him navigate social situations. Shore believes that every child, with or without autism, has unlimited potential and that we should provide support to access and build on children's strengths rather than emphasizing the improvement of weaknesses, which is where many therapies focus.

. . . .

WHAT IS A SOCIAL STORY?

Social Stories™ is an empirically validated, story-based intervention. A target behavior is identified and a written description of the situations under which the specific behavior is expected to occur is developed into a story. The goal of the story is to increase perspective-taking and to help the individual develop an understanding of how to behave in specific situations.

To help an autistic individual learn how to greet peers and teachers at school, as well as how to respond appropriately to others, a social story could be developed that describes this behavior.

For example:

When I see a friend or peer at school, there are different ways to greet them. I can say "Hi" or "Hello" or "What's up?". If they respond to me, I can stop and ask them, "How are you doing today?" It is important to smile when greeting someone and to respond with a smile when someone greets me.

. . . .

Other early indicators of autism are children who struggle with or avoid eye contact or who lack something referred to as *joint attention*. Joint attention is the ability to share focus on a common object and is a critical stage of nonverbal and social communication that develops during infancy. For example, if you're outside with an infant and there's a loud, startling noise, they will look to you to gauge the situation—is it something to fear or react to? They are sharing the incident with you and observing your "point of view." It's one of the earliest forms of communication, through which a child attempts to bring your attention to something or connect and share attention to an incident, object, or activity. This is a key developmental trait that children with autism often don't exhibit. If you are outside with an infant with autism, they may not react to the startling noise at all and may simply continue engaging in their activity.

This lack of attention to critical environmental cues and difficulty with social communication is a major characteristic of autism. When you walk into a place, your brain "reads" the environmental stimuli and cues to assess the setting and the situation. It's constantly scanning for and picking up on cues from your surroundings. Autistic individuals' brains do not assess settings and situations the same way most people's do. Things like the buzzing of a nearby fan or fluorescent light in a room may cause sensory overload for them, resulting in extremely uncomfortable feelings and the need to escape. Conversely, they may not attend to obvious noises or the calling of their name and may also struggle with the ability to pick up on social cues and interpret facial expressions. As a result, managing social situations becomes very challenging.

Our brains pick up on many nonverbal cues when we are interacting with people and we are unaware of most of them while they are happening. It's how we know, for example, when someone has become bored with a conversation, prompting us to change the topic or end the conversation. Our brains interpret eye movements, facial expressions, tone of voice, and body language to help us better read social situations. Some individuals with autism tend to interrupt and have difficulty starting or ending conversations. As such, individuals on the spectrum often come across as rude and abrupt, but they just don't understand or pick up on the unspoken rules that govern social interaction. This leads to trouble keeping friendships or holding down jobs, because their actions are often misinterpreted.

While these characteristics (lack of joint attention, difficulty picking up cues or expressing what they are experiencing) are broadly applicable to most individuals with autism, there are two main categories where deficits in functioning occur and are assessed for diagnosis; there is a high amount of variation between individuals in these areas. These categories are social communication and social interaction, and restricted interests and repetitive behaviors. A rating of severity is required within each category for diagnostic purposes.

According to the CDC, one-third of people with autism are nonverbal, around one-third have an intellectual disability, and the remaining population possesses typical ranges of intelligence and vocal communication.[26] It all depends on the individual and the manifestation of his or her autism.

Behavioral challenges are common among persons living with autism. These issues can range from meltdowns (that look like behavioral tantrums but have been described as being more like an anxiety attack) to serious, self-injurious behavior. Some behaviors are sensory in nature and may appear unusual to us, like rocking back and forth

---

26 Jon Baio, et al., "Prevalence of Autism Spectrum Disorder Among Children Aged 8 Years —Autism and Developmental Disabilities Monitoring Network, 11 Sites, United States, 2014," Surveillance Summaries 67, no. 6 (April 27, 2018): 1-23, http://dx.doi.org/10.15585/mmwr. ss6706a1.

repetitively, spinning objects repetitively, or flailing hands. These behaviors are known as "stimming." In more serious cases, individuals may engage in self-injurious behavior and hit themselves or bang their head against walls or other objects. Aggression should not be confused with stimming. Stimming provides sensory input and often counteracts anxiety and overstimulation. While many treatment programs try to eliminate stimming, individuals with autism will tell you that stimming has vital purposes, such as helping process information and experiences, process excitement, facilitate thinking, and alleviate anxiety.

What many people fail to understand about autism is that "acting out" or having a meltdown is a form of communication. Behavior is a form of communication for all of us, but individuals with autism don't respond to the same conversational or environmental cues and often lack the ability to adequately communicate when something is bothering them. A meltdown is an attempt to communicate illness, pain, fear, confusion, or that something in the environment is bothering them. Other times, an episode serves as sensory stimulation or release of anxiety.

Individuals with autism can also be very ritualistic and rigid in their daily routines. They tend to like things done in a certain way and in a specific order and thrive on structure and predictability. So, if you're driving someone with autism somewhere, that individual may want to follow the same route every time; they may even become very upset if you take a different street. Everything may be in patterns and rituals: how they arrange their toys, what they do before going to bed, or how they complete certain tasks. Many enjoy jobs where they can perform repetitive tasks. It's a reliance on familiar patterns and routines, whether at home, work, or school, that bring them comfort. Autistic individuals can become very upset and dysregulated when these patterns are broken.

Another behavioral component of autism is obsessive interest in very specific areas. For example, some may be obsessed with Disney movies and might memorize every line, every character, and every plot point. When these individuals enter social situations, they tend to only want to talk about this topic of interest. I worked with one child who was obsessed with toilets. He knew the make and manufacturer of every toilet and would ask people upon meeting them what kind of toilets they had in their home—not exactly appropriate conversation for most settings. These are the kind of traits that are often misunderstood and can be off-putting to people.

Sometimes individuals with autism possess savant-like skills. People used to wrongly believe that autism was synonymous with having an intellectual disability. Now we know that is only true for around a third of people with autism.[27] Certain individuals with autism are quite brilliant. There are nonverbal individuals who use computers or technology to communicate, have written books, and possess a high level of intellectual ability. Additionally, some even have unique abilities with data, computers, or memorization; they can listen to a piece of music and then sit down and play it perfectly. Stephen Wiltshire is an autistic artist who has become famous for his ability to draw detailed and to-scale replicas of cities after viewing the city very briefly from the skies while flying in a helicopter. For example, in 2001, Wiltshire appeared in a BBC documentary for which he flew above the city of London in a helicopter and thereafter completed a detailed drawing, in only three hours, of a four-square-mile area, including 200 structures and twelve historic landmarks.

27 Ibid.

He has completed panoramic drawings of many large cities around the globe entirely from memory.

Many people remember the movie *Rain Man,* where Tom Cruise's character uses his autistic brother's ability to count cards to win money gambling in Vegas. This is not out of the realm of possibility for some individuals, but it's important to note that autism does not come with super powers. While such savants do exist, it is wrong to assume that all autistic individuals have these types of special abilities.

HOW ABA PROGRAMS BREAK THROUGH THE COMMUNICATION BARRIER

The aim of intervention for individuals with autism should be to improve their ability to communicate, to adapt, and to learn the functional skills they require for optimal day-to-day living. In order to do this, we have to find ways to access learning and break through the communication barrier. Part of that is teaching these individuals to make associations.

Often, people with autism don't make the connection that language is a functional tool. They don't understand, for example, that if they say, "I want milk," someone will assist them in accessing milk. One of the goals of intervention is to help them make that association between language and communication skills and getting their needs addressed. This can be quite challenging, and individuals with autism often engage in aggressive behaviors or exhibit anxiety-related behaviors. You may watch them have a meltdown or bang their head, and you're left wondering, *Are they hungry or tired? Are they in pain? Are they trying to avoid something I have asked them to do?*

It really comes down to trying to understand the *function* of the behavior—what they're trying to accomplish or communicate—and then attempting to replace that behavior with a functional alternative that is safe and more productive for what they are hoping to accomplish. A child who wants to leave the room may just walk over and stare at the door, or they may experience a meltdown. The methodology of ABA provides for functional behavior assessments (FBA) and other tools which enable us to ascertain the function of a behavior. Once the function is understood, the therapist can teach the individual to use language or another form of communication to make a request, thereby making the connection between what they need and how to access this need. The goal is to use the child's motivation and needs to guide the learning while maintaining the consequence of the teaching as a natural and desired outcome. ABA is a technique used to reinforce and teach productive and functional behaviors to autistic individuals. I'll explain the details and inner workings of ABA later on in chapter 2.

The aim of intervention for individuals with autism should be to improve their ability to communicate, to adapt, and to learn the functional skills they require for optimal day-to-day living.

The communication barrier can be extremely frustrating for individuals with autism, their parents, and those who are working or living with them. It takes compassion, creativity, and a lot of patience to navigate the learning process.

I could give you my own advice for communicating with autistic individuals, but I think it's better to share some tips from a person who has written about this himself. Steve Summers, an autistic adult, wrote the following list for autismum.com, with the hopes of helping others better understand how best to communicate with individuals on the spectrum:

- We tend to take things literally and often have trouble reading between the lines. As a result, we may ask a lot of questions to clarify what is meant by something that you say. Don't be offended by this. It is our way of being sure that we understand what you are telling us.

- Please don't get offended by our communication style. We tend to be frank, honest, and matter-of-fact. Some people may interpret this as blunt or rude. We don't intend to be rude. Remember that communication is hard for us. Things that come naturally to you take extra effort for us.

- Please don't expect eye contact. We may be able to force eye contact, but it is not comfortable for us. Making eye contact takes a conscious effort. This effort may take away from listening and understanding what you are saying.

- Please don't speak down to us. Treat us as equals. We may sound flat or have an unusual tone to our voice. We may not speak with our voice at all. We may need to type our words. Please be patient with us. It may take us a while to formulate our answers.

- Please don't assume that we lack empathy or emotion.

- Please do NOT touch us without warning.

REFRAMING HOW WE LOOK AT AUTISM

In light of the increased prevalence of ASDs, the inadequate availability and accessibility of necessary services, support, and care for autistic individuals and their families is a national crisis. Clinicians, caregivers, teachers, researchers, and communities at large all have roles to play in addressing these issues. We simply cannot sit idly by while millions of individuals around the globe are left behind by society. We have a shared responsibility to take care of everyone in our communities. And, as a society comprised of individuals representing a wide range of neurological diversity, we can learn just as much from them as they can from us.

The term *neurodiversity* refers to the range of differences in individual brain function and behavioral traits. The neurodiversity approach argues that neurological differences like autism, ADHD, and others, are the result of natural variations within the human genome. The idea is to redefine the paradigm through which people view neurological disorders or differences—a paradigm which for a long time has viewed autistic individuals and others as "broken." A paradigm based on neurodiversity would view people with neurological disorders as *different, not broken* and would recognize and respect those differences just as any other human variation.

Most of the autistic individuals with whom I have spoken tell me they do not wish to be "made normal" and do not need to be cured; in fact, most tell me they take offense at this notion. Their autism cannot be separated from who they are—it is central to their identity. It is how their brain is wired, how it works, and how they perceive the world. What they do desire is help to better interact with their environments and the individuals within them. They need help learning how to communicate and navigate a world that is not built to accommodate the way their brains work. They need to learn to care for themselves and function independently—but they do not want to be fixed. Believing that they can, or should, be cured is a dangerous slope that has led to unrealistic expectations for the parents or caregivers of these individuals, which inevitably leads to frustration and disillusion when their child isn't cured.

This is especially true for parents facing the incredibly difficult situation of having a child who is severely affected by autism. In such instances, parents can struggle enormously, as children with such severe behaviors often cannot be left unattended and require twenty-four-hour care and support. Planning for their futures and addressing how they will be taken care of long-term is extremely worrisome for parents. The vast spectrum of autism conditions may make it difficult for the parents of children severely affected by autism to embrace the neurodiversity movement; some parents have expressed to me that when high-functioning individuals speak about neurodiversity, they are not speaking about the same world of autism that these parents are managing on a daily basis, as the issues they face daily differ enormously from those whose children will grow up to live independent lives.

Nonetheless, these parents do emphasize that the desire to find a cure and a cause shifts the focus away from what really matters today: quality of life. While researchers should and will continue to investigate these other aspects of ASD, the clinical emphasis should be on enhancing the quality of life of those living with autism. It is in this space that service providers and investors can do the most and have the greatest impact. Unfortunately, there are entire industries that have risen from pseudoscience, and there are advocacy movements that completely ignore quality of life in pursuit of cures or causes.

Even within the autism service industry, there exists a myopic lack of cooperation and a failure to collaborate in the measurement of long-term, meaningful outcomes.

In order to better serve those with autism and help them live richer lives and engage in meaningful civic participation, we must closely examine where we are today in terms of therapeutic outcomes and ask ourselves: How we can do better? In the following chapters, we will explore the current service provider landscape, discuss current interventions, understand why behavioral interventions are the "gold standard," examine outcomes, and share insights from those who have firsthand experience with it. We'll take a critical look at the outcomes autism service providers are producing and make the case that the time has come for the industry to evolve.

CHAPTER 2

BREAKING DOWN AUTISM INTERVENTIONS

W hen we look at services for autism, there is a wide range of available treatment choices, and it can be challenging to know what to choose. If you search the Internet for "autism interventions," as any parent of a newly diagnosed child would likely do, you are inundated with a myriad of options for interventions ranging from intensive ABA and behavioral intervention programs, to other types of interventions, to "alternative" treatments such as vitamin therapy regimens, hyperbaric oxygen therapy, medication regimens, chelation therapy, and other "fad" treatments.

How are parents and investors to know which interventions work, and which interventions are backed by science with documented evidence of efficacy? It is first important to differentiate between evidence-based practice, such as applied behavioral analysis (ABA), and non-evidence-based practices.

FAQ:

WHY IS EARLY INTERVENTION SO IMPORTANT?

The first five years of a child's development are critical for many reasons. This is a period of rapid learning in all areas of growth and it is vital to capitalize on this period of development.

The brain is still developing at birth and experiences during the first few years of life have lasting effects on the development of the brain and its functioning. Interactions between a child, her environment, and caregivers are essential to this process.

Brain plasticity: "Neurons that fire together, wire together."

An infant is born with eighty-five billion neurons which transmit information forming neural networks, a series of interconnected neurons. As a baby experiences something in his or her environment, a strong neural connection is made. If this experience is repeated, the connection becomes stronger and reinforced. If the experience is not repeated, the connection is "pruned". As we grow in the first years of life, many neural connections that do not prove useful and functional are pruned.

Children with developmental disorders and learning disabilities have neural connections that are not "useful" causing them to have difficulties with communication and other skills. The sooner we intervene and offer learning opportunities by which the brain can form new, appropriate, and functional connections, the stronger and deeper those behaviors and skills can be consolidated in the brain.

This understanding of the brain's plasticity is particularly relevant to understanding the importance of intensive early intervention. The brain can still learn and adapt in adolescence and adulthood, but it takes longer.

What is agreed upon is that early intervention is critical for children diagnosed with ASD, as well as for children determined to be at risk for ASD and other developmental disorders. However, what continues to be prevalent in the field of autism intervention is a myriad of treatment options, many not backed by evidence to support their efficacy. The vast spectrum of autism (and the characteristics and conditions associated with it), the lifelong nature of the disability, and the debate surrounding cause and cure have led to many types of interventions advertising remarkable results that parents often latch onto in a desperate attempt to see quick and positive outcomes. These treatments, as well as many parent groups that advocate their use, often perpetuate the fear and stigma associated with autism and the idea that it can be fixed and cured. Parents mostly lack the knowledge to differentiate between evidence-based and pseudoscientific treatments and should be wary of anyone who says they can cure an incurable disorder.

EVIDENCE-BASED INTERVENTION

We know from scientific exploration that behavioral interventions based on the principles of ABA, as well as some other treatment options, are highly effective for autism, and I will go into detail explaining those in this chapter. Even with this agreement in the scientific community, the rate at which the prevalence of autism has grown has led to a great demand for services, not all of which are of the quality and clinical utility that the scientific process of ABA would prescribe.

The field of ABA-based service delivery has become diluted to the extent that one provider who says they deliver "ABA" services may be referring to a program that adheres to the principles and technology of the science of ABA, while another may simply be referring to a single teaching technique, such as discrete trial training (a method within ABA, described later). Others still may be referring to a diluted version of ABA, where the program is not based on a comprehensive clinical model or the collection of meaningful data to guide programmatic modifications and relevant outcomes. Such versions also often lack in quality assurance measures.

Specific criteria need to be met when research is conducted to evaluate the efficacy of an intervention method. At least two studies, conducted by independent researchers, need to demonstrate that the intervention has superior outcomes to other established treatments or a placebo. If group studies are not feasible—as is often the case in autism intervention, due to the extremely heterogeneous population—several single-subject design studies must demonstrate those same criteria.

According to standards set by the American Psychological Association (APA), efficacy should be evaluated in terms of both effectiveness of the clinical intervention (evaluating the strength of the causal relationship between an intervention and the disorder) and clinical utility ("consideration of the available research evidence and clinical consensus regarding the generalizability, feasibility, and costs and benefits of the intervention").[28] The APA defines *evidence-based practice* as "the integration of the best available research with clinical expertise in the context of patient characteristics, culture, and preferences" and states that "generally, evidence derived from clinically relevant research on psychological practices should be based on systematic reviews, reasonable effect sizes, statistical and clinical significance, and a body of supporting evidence."

In 2006, Green and associates conducted a survey of 111 different treatments for autism.[29] On average, parents were utilizing seven treatments at any given time, rendering it almost impossible to determine which treatment was responsible for the change in their child's skills and abilities. While scientifically unsupported treatments may initially be deemed beneficial by individual parents, they often turn out to be a waste of time, resources, money, and considerable effort. Some of the treatments have adverse side effects, and many have potential long-term deleterious effects. The safety of treatments should continuously be evaluated, and it is always of value to consider the time potentially wasted in unsupported treatments versus supported treatments.

When looking to understand evidence-based interventions (called *established interventions*), there are specific studies and analyses that have been conducted to determine which interventions are evidence-based and which are not. The National Standards Project (Phase 1 and Phase 2) is a review of behavioral and educational peer-reviewed intervention studies using quantitative research designs involving individuals with ASD and published in peer-reviewed journals. Refer to the chart included in the further reading and infor-

---

28 APA Presidential Task Force on Evidence-Based Practice, "Evidence-Based Practice in Psychology," *American Psychologist* 61, no. 4 (May–June 2006): 271–285.

29 VA Green, KA Pituch, J Itchon et al. "Internet survey of treatments used by parents of children with autism," *Research in Developmental Disabilities* 27, no. 1 (2006): 70–84.

mation section, which describes the three categories of interventions: established interventions, emerging interventions (interventions with some research to support them, but not sufficient evidence to classify them as evidence-based), and unestablished interventions (those with no scientific support of efficacy). Phase 1 of the National Standards Project occurred in 2009, and Phase 2 occurred in 2015. With the addition of new studies reviewed in Phase 2, some interventions moved from one category to another (for example, with additional evidence, an intervention may be moved from the classification of an emerging intervention to an established intervention). In addition, data from an environmental scan of the scientific evidence regarding the efficacy, safety, and availability of services and supports for individuals with ASD conducted for the Centers for Medicare and Medicaid Services are included.[30] For more information, please refer to the provided chart in the further reading and information section.

While many of the established interventions are based on behavioral principles and could be considered to be one category, they are broken into different interventions to distinguish between them. This is important. They may appear similar at first glance, but they are different and represent how a well-rounded clinical program is comprised. Some of these programs focus on language, while others focus on social skills or independent living skills. Some target core, specific, critical developmental skills in very young children, such as joint attention,[31] while others target skills important in adolescence.

---

30 Julie Young, et al., "Autism Spectrum Disorders (ASDs) Services: Final Report on Environmental Scan," IMPAQ International, last modified March 9, 2010, http://www.autismhandbook.org/images/8/8a/ASD_Services_Environmental_Scan.pdf.

31 Research has shown that children who engage a parent or caregiver in shared communication, such as directing their attention to an event of interest or pointing to an object, learn language faster.

It is important to know and understand them separately, because programs tailored to the unique needs of an individual must select specific interventions from a body of approved and established options. This is a very important aspect of high-quality interventions following best practice guidelines.

While other therapies (speech therapy, occupational therapy, physical therapy, and other modalities) have been impactful for individuals with all types of special needs, this book focuses on ABA and behavioral interventions, because this category is considered the gold standard of treatment in autism intervention. That is because the science of ABA is empirically validated, with decades of research to support its efficacy; thus, the intervention is funded by most payers. In this chapter, we will explore current interventions and examine why ABA and behavior interventions are at the forefront of autism treatment. Then, later in the book, we will explore the outcomes of such intervention.

WHAT IS APPLIED BEHAVIOR ANALYSIS (ABA)?

ABA is an evidence-based, scientific discipline that focuses on objectively defining behaviors of social significance and intervening to improve those behaviors while also demonstrating a relationship between the applied intervention and the behavioral improvement. The approach includes methods such as observation, quantification, and controlled experimentation.

An example of a socially significant behavior is making a request to meet a need, such as asking for food. Using the techniques and strategies of ABA, we teach individuals that when they ask for something, either verbally or using another form of functional communication, a direct and natural response is received. Learned behavioral responses like this are a way in which we all form connections and learn to navigate the world; individuals with autism just have a more difficult time in certain areas.

For example, we've likely all seen a typical child throwing a temper tantrum after their parent has denied them something at the grocery store. What we may not understand is that a tantrum is a way of communicating, especially among children whose verbal skills are not yet developed. If a child sees some candy they want, and their parents tell them no, the child may act up. Sometimes, parents will give in just to calm the child and make their lives easier in that moment. However, by doing so, they have reinforced the unwanted behavior. The next time the child wants candy, they are far more likely to "throw a tantrum," because they have learned to associate that behavior with getting what they want. However, if the parent stays firm and consistently does not reward the behavioral outburst by giving the child candy, the child will not make a connection between excessive behaviors and receiving candy.

The same principle applies to an autistic child who, to give a simplistic example, is biting his hand because he wants candy and doesn't understand how to vocalize that desire. If you give the child candy, you are reinforcing and strengthening the undesirable and unsafe behavior, essentially teaching him that biting his hand will result in access to candy. Reinforcement strengthens behaviors and shapes future behavior, whether those behaviors are considered positive or negative.

Even as adults, we do this all the time in our interpersonal interactions. If a person gives their significant other a compliment, such as telling them that they like their hair a certain way, their partner is more likely to wear it that way again. The compliment reinforces the behavior, and because they likely enjoy compliments from their significant other, they will increase the behavior. We are constantly shaping behavior in our personal relationships and when interacting with our environments—we just don't recognize it.

With children, the goal is to teach functional behaviors. We want to ignore unwanted or inappropriate behaviors and reinforce functional, appropriate behaviors such as intentional requests. Intentional requests can take many forms, including pointing, sign language, a verbal request, or communication via the use of technology. If a mother stays firm and doesn't reward her son with candy when he is acting out, she can teach him that she will respond to a verbal request or a more appropriate, less disruptive communication. At that point, the child understands that he needs to use words (or another form of functional communication) to get candy. It's about teaching the child and shaping his behavior by ignoring the actions you don't want and rewarding those you do.

This is the basic premise behind intervening in behavior and teaching responses using the principles of ABA, which, in the right hands, can be a powerful, positive tool for helping children with autism, as well as others, learn how to better communicate and interact with their environments. However, ABA in the wrong hands can be detrimental and even counterproductive. A key aspect to ABA is analysis: the demonstration that the intervention we employed was actually responsible for the improvement of the behavior. This requires ongoing and meaningful data collection and measurement of outcomes, without which we have lost the evidence-based part of the discipline. For clinicians and investors, it's important to understand the discipline, its history and evolution, and how it can and should be applied to create outcomes that are relevant to helping individuals with autism function in society.

THE SHIFT AWAY FROM INSTITUTIONALIZATION

Decades ago, before autism was properly understood and prior to the development of treatment options in the field, institutionalization was the common response to individuals living with autism and other disabilities. In many ways, these institutions were a place where human beings who were deemed broken or too sick to live in society were locked away. Often, families were told to forget about their child and move on with their lives. Some institutions provided for basic human needs, but others were grim and abusive places. Individuals with mental disabilities of all types were often strapped to beds for the majority of their days or locked in rooms and left in their own waste. It was an unfortunate and regrettable response from a society that did not understand and held no compassion for individuals who were viewed as less than human.

My first experience with an institutional environment came while I was an undergraduate student. My psychology professor, Dr. John Lutzker, invited me to do a practicum study at Camarillo State Hospital. The goal was to see if we could influence and alter staff behavior to increase staff engagement with patients and then examine the impact increased engagement had on patients. To that end, our work focused on the staff more so than the patients, employing behaviorally based strategies to improve staff interactions.

Typically, the staff spent most of their time in the staff room engaged with each other. Post-intervention, the staff did become more likely to play games or have brief conversations with patients. The collateral effect was that patients were more engaged, more alert, and slightly more involved in the world around them. That was my first hands-on work with ABA and the power of antecedents and consequences on shaping behavior. It was also my first real look into the institutionalization of people with developmental disabilities and the effects of what was essentially warehousing individuals. People were woken up in the morning, fed, and had their basic hygiene needs attended to. Then they would be led into a room where they would sit all day, watching TV or staring blankly, before being brought back to their rooms after dinner, when it was time to sleep. No one was attempting to engage with them, and there was very little effort in terms of teaching them skills. People had practically given up on these individuals, who lived day-to-day with very little to stimulate their brains.

Thankfully, times have changed, and institutionalization is no longer recommended for most individuals living with autism. It was through the tireless efforts of parent advocates, who refused to allow institutionalization to be the only option for their children, and scientists and researchers developing treatment options through which new therapeutic opportunities became available, that enabled children to attend school and remain at home with their families. That, combined with investigative reporting, helped put an end to unnecessary institutionalization.

The development of ABA and its application to individuals with all kinds of developmental disabilities, including autism, provided a framework that would begin to shift the paradigm of how the future for children with developmental disabilities was viewed.

FAQ:

WHAT IS THE IDEAL ENVIRONMENT FOR DELIVERY OF SERVICES: CENTER-BASED OR HOME-BASED?

Some of the most frequent questions I am asked about in regard to providing services for children with autism are: What are best practices for service delivery? Are home-based services better than center-based services? Is forty hours a week better than twenty, always?

There is no perfect, clean answer to these questions.

There are many factors that impact the quality and outcomes of services, as well as the costs and clinical operations. For example, it may be more cost effective to provide center-based services because your staff members are not driving to client's homes. Center-based services can be more clinically effective, in some respects, because you can maximize utilization and provide more consistent supervision and ongoing training; however, you are limited to how many clients you can see per day based on the capacity of your centers. Another important consideration is the clinical efficacy of interventions and the age of the child, as learning in the natural environment and parental involvement are pivotal to long-term success.

In addition, funding sources and legislation often dictate the location of service delivery, intensity of intervention hours, and the operational design of programs. An examination of the multiple factors and variables involved determines the most cost and clinically effective practice.

Through the science of ABA and the development of other treatments for individuals with developmental disorders, many breakthroughs have been made. Most notably, a thriving autism services provider market exists, empowering, aiding, and educating individuals with autism. Due in large part to these scientific advancements, institutionalization is no longer the predominant approach to care for autistic individuals, and that has helped change the way society views individuals with autism or other disabilities. But we must not settle for where we are today or assume there is no room for improvement. Individuals with autism and other disabilities will tell you how much harder they have to work to create the lives they want for themselves. We can support them in achieving the lives they long for by molding society into one that is more understanding of its members who are uniquely different and providing autistic individuals with comprehensive services including speech and occupational therapies, education, and community awareness and acceptance.

While other therapies have been impactful for individuals with all types of special needs (speech therapy, occupational therapy, physical therapy, and other modalities), this book focuses on ABA and behavioral interventions because this category is considered the gold standard of treatment in autism intervention. That is because the science is empirically validated with decades of research to support its efficacy and thus the intervention is funded by most payers. In this chapter, we will explore current interventions and examine why ABA and behavior interventions are at the forefront of autism treatment. Then, later in the book, we will explore the outcomes of such intervention.

THE EVOLUTION OF ABA

ABA can only be fully understood in the context of the research experiments, findings, and philosophies from which it originates. ABA has a long history that begins early in the twentieth century with a philosophical switch of the targeted subject matter for study in psychology from mental process (Freud) to observable behavior (Watson). Watson promoted the direct observation of behavior to understand the relationship between stimuli and the responses they evoked and made a strong case for the study of behavior. In 1938, B. F. Skinner published *The Behavior of Organisms*, which formally launched the experimental branch of behavior analysis and defined two types of behavior: operant and respondent.

The origins of ABA trace back to researchers from the University of Kansas and the University of Washington. Among these were Donald Baer, Montrose Wolfe, and Todd Risley, who developed many strategies and technologies for interventions that shaped the principles of ABA. In 1968, they founded the *Journal of Applied Behavioral Analysis*, a journal dedicated to publishing research on behavioral analysis.

. . . .

Baer, Wolf, and Risley published a seminal paper in 1968, defining the criteria for assessing the adequacy of research and practice in ABA. This paper is still used as the standard description of ABA and defines ABA as having seven characteristics:

→ APPLIED (FOCUSING ON SOCIALLY SIGNIFICANT BEHAVIORS)

→ BEHAVIORAL (OBJECTIVELY MEASURED BEHAVIOR)

→ ANALYTIC (DEMONSTRATION THAT THE INTERVENTION WAS ACTUALLY RESPONSIBLE FOR THE CHANGE IN BEHAVIOR)

→ TECHNOLOGICAL (THE DESCRIPTION OF THE RESEARCH MUST BE CLEAR AND DETAILED SO THAT IT CAN BE REPLICATED)

→ CONCEPTUALLY SYSTEMATIC (THE METHODS SHOULD BE GROUNDED IN BEHAVIORAL PRINCIPLES)

→ EFFECTIVE (THE INTERVENTION MUST PRODUCE AN EFFECT THAT IS LARGE ENOUGH FOR PRACTICAL USE)

→ GENERAL (BEHAVIOR ANALYSTS SHOULD AIM FOR INTERVENTIONS THAT ARE GENERALLY APPLICABLE, WORK IN MULTIPLE ENVIRONMENTS, AND HAVE LONG-LASTING EFFECTS)

. . . .

I had the privilege of learning from some of these seminal figures in the ABA field while working toward my doctorate at the University of Kansas. I was part of a joint doctoral program and had the opportunity to study with Don Baer as part of his research team, as well as to take classes from Montrose Wolf. While moving to Kansas just a few years after immigrating to Los Angeles and starting to adjust to living in California meant another upheaval for me, I was encouraged by my undergraduate advisor and now lifelong mentor, Dr. John Lutzker, to take advantage of the tremendous opportunity to work with and learn from the inspirational and influential scholars in our field. I had the unique experience of having three "generations" of Kansas graduates on my dissertation advisory committee. John; his advisor for his doctorate, Jim Sherman; and Jim's advisor, Don Baer, all mentored me and guided my doctoral studies.

While Baer, Wolf, and Risley had established the foundation of the true application of behavior analysis, as well as the development of many technologies and strategies within ABA, the implementation of ABA as we know it today in the field of autism was shaped by the work of several other pioneers, the most prolific of which was Dr. Ivar Lovaas, whose legacy is applying the work of ABA to autism. He established the UCLA Young Autism Project while teaching at the University of California, Los Angeles, and devoted nearly half a century to groundbreaking research and practice aimed at improving the lives of children with autism and their families.

Dr. Lovaas began his work in institutional settings where treatments using Freudian approaches were being used. Individuals engaging in self-injury were often hugged and given love, as it was theorized they were acting out toward their parents, who did not, or perhaps could not, love them. This was a very unfortunate initial theory that blamed the parents for their children's autism. As recently as 1960, Dr.

To learn more about the history of ABA, see the further reading and information section.

Leo Kanner described parents of autistic children as "happening to defrost enough to produce a child," hence the term, "refrigerator parent." Bruno Bettelheim promoted the use of the "refrigerator mother" theory of autism, which held that autism was a product of parental neglect. He felt that the children would benefit from a "parentectomy" (i.e., removal from the home) and be better served in clinical or institutional settings. This marked the pinnacle of autism being viewed as a disorder of faulty parenting.

Dr. Lovaas subsequently introduced ABA strategies and techniques to individuals engaging in severe forms of self-injury. These were cases where the self-injury was severe enough to cause premature death or a significant decrease in quality of life. Treatment sought to reinforce positive, or "appropriate," behavior and discourage or punish self-injurious behavior. Loving praise and hugs were given at times when patients were not engaging in self-injury, as a way of reinforcing the preferred behavior. The data collected from these experiments indicated that, on most occasions, self-injury was a result of prior learning, not traumatic childhood events, and could be modified by altering the contingencies following their occurrence. As self-injury was acquired via association with subsequent positive social attention, and the self-injury was reduced when positive social attention was removed (subsequent to the behavior), attention was identified as a primary motivator and the function of the behavior.

Lovaas then began the controversial use of punishment as a deterrent to harmful behaviors. While most consider the use of electric shock on individuals with intellectual delays to be cruel or archaic, its effectiveness in reducing self-injurious behaviors in those initial explorations could not be disputed. It's important to remember that these self-injurious behaviors were debilitating and often life-threatening. These individuals were extremely self-injurious and were physically restrained almost constantly to prevent them from harming themselves. At the time, it was considered cutting-edge work and changed the direction of treatment.

However, the use of punishment has plagued Lovaas's legacy and has become associated for some with the science of ABA, even though today, most applications of ABA are in natural environments without the use of aversive techniques. If the use of shock is necessary as an intervention, strong safeguards are in place to closely monitor its use and prevent any adverse side effects. Controversy aside, Lovaas's work marks much of the shift in treatment for autism on a larger scale, from a Freudian-theory-based practice to one based solely on using contingences to alter behaviors, conducting empirical evaluations, and utilizing reliable data collection.

> For two case study examples of my early work with ABA in the field, please refer to the further reading and information section at the end of the book.

THE ORIGINS OF THE APPLICATION OF ABA TO AUTISM

In the mid-1960s, Dr. Lovaas developed a program designed to teach language to children with autism to help them avoid institutionalization. Some of the children received up to forty hours per week of direct, one-on-one instruction for an average of thirteen months. In 1973, Lovaas's first published study showed significant improvements in children with autism. Despite the small sample size, this study was the first to demonstrate that young children with autism could learn at an accelerated rate. This led to new and exciting parameters for treatment being discovered and helped establish his program for children with autism, Early Intensive Behavior Intervention (EIBI).

Lovaas's data demonstrated that the strengths of his program were a structured, intensive, full-time teaching environment requiring between twenty and sixty hours per week of intervention for at least two to three years. The "Lovaas Model" was very structured, repetitive, adult-led, and sometimes used punishment (such as slapping children in the face and yelling), that is, when these procedures were implemented there was a decrease in inappropriate behaviors. Results showed that participants largely failed to generalize their learning outside of the clinic setting. This led to Lovaas modifying his clinical recommendations and ultimately advocating for teaching children at home, using parents as therapists. Subsequent studies attempted to address the shortfalls demonstrated by his initial study.

In a subsequent study ("The 1987 Study"), sixty children were divided into three groups. The "experimental" group received forty hours per week of intervention. "Control group one" received ten hours per week of the same intervention as the experimental group, along with special education. "Control group two" received special education only. The data on the group that received forty hours per week (for two to six years) reported that 47 percent of the children became "indistinguishable from their peers" or had the "best outcome," whereas the other groups experienced little to moderate progress, with only one child achieving the "best outcome."

Following the 1987 study, the Lovaas Model of Applied Behavior Analysis, which became the EIBI model, gained popularity and became more widely implemented. This model has evolved and today consists of a combination of structured and naturalistic approaches offered intensively (thirty-five to forty-plus hours per week) and including facilitated peer play and support in school environments. Some controversy surrounds this model because of methodological limitations in the research and the use of the term "recovered" in the original study, referring to individuals with autism as having recovered from their disorder.

The reason it is important to understand the research conducted by Lovaas is because of the impact his research and findings had on autism intervention. Intensive early intervention programs were launched as a result of his outcomes, despite the fact that the number of participants was small. Parent advocacy groups became very staunch advocates of this method of intervention, some telling parents that if they did not give their children the "Lovaas method" of treatment they would be harming them for life. Even today, despite the movement toward neurodiversity and the desire for acceptance of autistic individuals for who they are, some behavioral service providers promote their interventions with promises of "recovery" and making children "indistinguishable from their peers," using the Lovaas research from 1987 as their platform for doing so.

To be clear, I am not an advocate of the original Lovaas method; it is too rigid and unnatural. Nor do I advocate for forty-plus-hour programs for every child. Lovaas's work created an important foundation for the implementation of ABA in autism, but his initial approach also fostered a mind-set among parents and providers that intervention must be very structured, intensive, rigid, and, for some, that ABA is aversive by design. It's important to discuss his work, but it's also important to note that the delivery of ABA in the home and community settings has evolved quite significantly to promote generalization of learning and become more family-focused and naturalistic. As important as his method was in the formation of the application of ABA in autism, it is not a one-size-fits-all intervention for every child with autism.

TYPES OF ABA INTERVENTION

While Lovaas's research formed much of the foundation for the application of ABA to autism, simultaneously in the 1970s and 1980s, other researchers at universities and clinics around the country began to develop other treatments and methods of teaching based on the principles of ABA. Discrete trial training (DTT), one of the teaching methods developed by Lovaas at UCLA, is a method of teaching in which the adult uses adult-directed, massed trail instruction, clear contingencies, reinforcers, and lots of repetition to teach skills.[32] Others developed more naturalistic techniques to teach functional skills and improve behaviors using more child-directed, naturalistic, and play-based methods. For example, pivotal response treatment* (PRT), an evidence-based intervention developed by Drs. Robert and Lynn Koegel, targets important areas of a child's development, such as motivation, responsivity to multiple cues, self-management, and social initiations, to teach communication and other functional skills. Please refer to the chart on different types of interventions found in the further reading and information section for more details on these interventions.

---

32 Massed trial instruction is an adult-directed teaching method whereby the same skill is taught repeatedly in a sequence. Clear contingencies refers to the fact that the learning sequence of each trial has a clear beginning (instruction), middle (response) and end (consequence).

ESTABLISHED INTERVENTION BASED
ON BEHAVIORAL PRINCIPLES (ABA)

DISCRETE TRIAL TRAINING (DTT)

- Therapist-directed.
- Structured teaching: home or school setting. Typically conducted one-on-one between therapist and child.
- Follows a structured curriculum largely targeting the child's deficits.
- Reinforcement is not necessarily connected to the activity or skill being taught.
- Generally only used during an intervention session.
- Recommended 25-40+ hours/week delivered by a professional.

PIVOTAL RESPONSE TREATMENT (PRT®)

- Child-directed.
- Naturalistic teaching strategy adaptable to any setting: home, school, playground, shopping mall, extracurricular activities; includes family members, friends & peers.
- Play and activity based—targets pivotal areas of a child's development such as motivation, responsivity to multiple cues, self-management & social initiations. Tailored to meet child's needs.
- Reinforcement is directly related to the activity and skill being taught.
- Caregivers in the child's natural environment empowered to use PRT® throughout the day—"lifestyle" vs. a "teaching method
- Recommended minimum 25 hours/week— delivered by caregivers and professionals

Established Intervention.

Based on principles of applied behavior analysis (ABA).

Empirically validated.

Uses positive reinforcement.

Used to teach and shape meaningful skills and behaviors.

Benefits all age groups.

WHAT SHOULD INTERVENTION LOOK LIKE?

One of the first children with whom I worked as a doctoral student in an autism treatment program was a four-year-old, mostly nonverbal boy named Jason. Occasionally, he would babble or speak random words but almost never in an obvious attempt to make a request or communicate his needs. He would typically request something by pointing and gesturing. Further complicating the communication barrier, Jason would experience many meltdowns. In an effort to find a way to create effective communication with Jason, I discussed his communication patterns and behavior with his parents. I wanted to know what they thought would motivate him, as well as the areas of difficulty they were experiencing.

During our initial conversation, his parents brought out a variety of Jason's preferred items, including a juice box. Jason immediately became interested in it. I used this to demonstrate a basic, naturalistic therapeutic technique to his parents. When a child is interested in an object, activity, or action, this interest can be used as motivation to elicit responses. To show his parents how this works, I partially covered the juice box with my hand, looked at Jason, and said, "juice." Jason's attention remained held by the juice box and I repeated this several times. After a few repetitions, Jason made an utterance that barely approximated the sound of the word "juice." It wasn't clearly articulated, but it was intentional, and his gaze was focused on me and the box of juice. Immediately, I handed him the juice box and let him take a sip. Once he had taken a sip, I told him it was my turn and took the juice box back. He was not pleased, but his motivation to gain access was key. Once again, I blocked access to the juice box and said "juice," waiting for him to repeat it. He repeated the utterance much more quickly this time, and he was given the juice box for another sip, rewarding his response. Once he became familiar with the pattern, he began to understand that his making an utterance that sounded like "juice" resulted in access to juice. This exchange became a game between us, and he started saying "yoos" over and over again until the juice box was finished.

We moved onto the floor, where his parents had set out a variety of toys. He quickly became interested in playing with a wooden train set. I repeated the same technique, blocking access and saying the word "train." Then I waited for him to repeat the word (or an approximation of it) before giving him access to the toy. He quickly made the connection and started repeating approximations of my words far more rapidly and with much more enthusiasm. What was most important was that his parents saw how to elicit verbal requests from him and teach him the connection between verbal language and communication, essentially beginning the process of breaking the communication barrier between them and their son.

The socially significant behavior I initially identified in Jason was making a request to meet a need: asking for juice. We demonstrated for him that saying the word "juice"—or as he said it, "yoos"—was directly linked to receiving juice, a direct and natural response or reinforcement to his request.

We had limited time to work with this family, so our program was completely focused on working with the parents, who eagerly learned the strategies we taught them and went on to use them consistently with Jason. About seven months after we first met, Jason's mom called me to say that he had started calling her "mama" when he wanted her attention. It may seem like a small step, but to a mother who had been unable to verbally communicate with her son for the first four and a half years of his life, it was a huge breakthrough. She said she never thought she would ever hear him communicate intentionally, let alone call her "mama." This progress meant the world to her, and it was a moment I have always remembered.

The techniques I used with Jason are based on PRT, which is a naturalistic intervention derived from ABA. At the company I cofounded, we demonstrated considerable success using PRT as a large component of our model and teaching methodology due to its naturalistic approach and focus on family needs and dynamics. Many ABA programs out there today are still using very rigid, regimented, adult-directed programs, which follow strict, cookie-cutter curricula and prescribe a specific order of steps and learning. One prescription, for example, is to teach a child to make eye contact first, then to put his hands in his lap, then to do a high-five, then to clap, then to identify body parts, and so on.

I don't believe this is the most effective approach, as there is no "one-size-fits-all." Intervention should be based on following the child's lead and motivation, teaching important skills in the context of natural daily routines. Programs need to be individualized to serve the needs of each child and his or her family. There is a place for some structured teaching when applicable, but the key is customization. We accomplished consistently strong outcomes by operating on this premise, as it allows for more individualization and focuses on what the child actually needs rather than what a program says he or she should learn.

> *What was most important was that his parents saw how to elicit verbal requests from him and teach him the connection between verbal language and communication, essentially beginning the process of breaking the communication barrier between them and their son.*

While it's important to figure out how to engage a child so that he or she wants to learn, we should be emphasizing functional and age-appropriate skills that will serve the child in the long-term. That requires assessing the skills a child has, how old the child is, and what the goals are for the child's future. Rather than following a standard curriculum, appropriate goals need to be set based on the child's functional needs and natural inclinations. For example, if a child is twelve years old, is it productive to spend a year or more trying to teach them the difference between red and blue? I think it's far more important to teach them crucial life skills, like how to tie their shoes, dress themselves, and shower independently. People can get lost in the curricula rather than targeting the goals whose outcomes will yield optimal benefits and an improved quality of life to the child and will serve the ultimate purpose of achieving maximal independence.[33]

ABA service providers can also lose sight of the individual by focusing too much on the curricula. For example, individuals with autism often express how physically uncomfortable eye contact is for them, yet this is one of the primary skills taught in intervention programs, because it is so important for social interaction. The inclusion of this skill as one of the first to be taught in intervention programs often overlooks the stress and anxiety this causes autistic individuals. Individuals might not have the ability to tell us how anxious it makes them, but that doesn't mean it isn't stressful for them. There are techniques by which making eye contact can be taught that are significantly less stressful than a rigid, structured teaching format of *demanding* eye contact. We have to remember that these individuals are having human experiences and managing stress and anxiety most often without the tools to do so. Focusing too much on a structured curriculum tends to undermine this consideration.

As one examines and better understands the autism service provider landscape, it becomes evident that as businesses providing services for autism have rapidly emerged across the United States, there are many and varying interpretations of ABA. DTT is often disliked for its rigidity and structure and has become widely misunderstood by society and by some providers to represent the entirety

---

33 Nouchine Hadjikhani et al., "Look me in the eyes: constraining gaze in the eye-region provokes abnormally high subcortical activation in autism," *Scientific Reports* 7, no. 3163 (June 9, 2017) doi:10.1038/s41598-017-03378-5.

of ABA, as opposed to a teaching technique within ABA. As a result, some immediately reject the notion of providing ABA services for their child because of the negative connotations and associations with DTT's teaching format, and the reputation of ABA services has suffered.

Intervention should be based on following the child's lead and motivation, teaching important skills in the context of natural daily routines. Programs need to be individualized to serve the needs of each child and his or her family.

Many fail to appreciate that ABA is a systematic approach to changing behavior, which teaches skills with many strategies and techniques. A comprehensive program will include a variety of techniques as interventions and, if part of a high-quality program, will be customized and modified to meet the individual's needs as they change.

THE NATURALISTIC APPROACH

One would expect that the best therapies are naturalistic and occur in familiar environments. Common sense tells us that sitting in a clinic room at a desk for eight hours a day is not the natural environment for a two-year-old. For ABA to be effective and fun for a young child, it should look like play. Most of the time, that means getting down onto the floor with the child, going outside, or engaging during mealtime or some other activity of daily living. That does not mean ABA isn't a complex and technological program. A good, solid ABA program is extremely complex and intense to run, but it should be fun and engaging for the child.

Building on the best of ABA and interventions such as PRT, what we did at our company was create a naturalistic model that incorporated primary caregivers, including babysitters, mothers, fathers, and grandparents. We engaged whoever the primary caregivers were in that child's life and taught them strategies as well. Our goal was to establish consistency so that when we, the interventionists, were not present, the child was still receiving the same therapeutic techniques and strategies from caregivers in their environment. This essentially transforms the intervention from a session-based experience to a living, breathing, full-time program. It's ongoing, consistent, and naturalistic rather than relying solely on a behavior interventionist to sit with the child only a few hours a day.

When the intervention becomes a 24/7 program, the outcomes are substantially better. And because we were teaching parents, teachers, and caregivers to use these techniques, we were able to achieve remarkable outcomes with fewer intervention hours provided. The child lives the program and has more consistent applications throughout their day, no matter where they are or whom they are with.

Part of this naturalistic approach is based on normal family or home life routines. It has to be family-focused, meaning it has to take the family's needs into account. If a mother has had no sleep, and she's suffering from a great deal of stress, she's not going to be able to engage in parent support sessions very well. So, addressing the needs of the whole family and the caregivers is just as critical and cannot be ignored. Effective intervention needs to be able to adapt, determine what the family's capacity is, and address the needs of all involved.

Through a naturalistic, ecobehavioral approach, the child plays a key role in developing their own skills, with the interventionist following their interests, inclinations, and wants rather than being forced to follow a rigid curriculum behind a desk, often in an unnatural setting. It teaches them in their natural environment and follows their cues as to what can be used to motivate them. With the entire family involved, the program becomes a consistent, embedded part of the child's life.

. . . .

The "eco" in ecobehavioral refers to the social ecology created by how each family member affects the other members within the family. "Behavioral" represents the methodology of treating and addressing issues in the environment in which they occur.

By way of example, when a child is diagnosed with autism, the impact of that diagnosis affects everyone in the family system. Typically, one parent gives up working in order to take on the day-to-day responsibility of caring for the child, arranging all the interventions and appointments, and advocating for that child. That often brings financial hardship and pressure to the working parent to provide financially. Siblings in the family are affected by the amount of time, attention, and resources that need to be devoted to the affected child. Often, the family is less able to participate in family and community activities due to the communication, social, and behavioral challenges experienced by the child with autism.

An ecobehavioral approach to services adopts a family-focused approach taking into consideration all these factors and examines how intervention can support the family in all areas of challenge and difficulty.

. . . .

ACCEPTANCE OF ABA

Through the work of individuals like Ivar Lovaas, Robert and Lynn Koegel, and many others, different approaches aimed at intervening in behavior and teaching skills were developed for autism. The name "applied behavioral analysis" describes an intensive teaching program emphasizing the importance of analyzing and understanding behavior as an interaction with one's environment and teaching new and functional skills using the techniques and strategies of ABA. Clinical reports and research examining the efficacy of ABA have determined that the benefit of ABA-based interventions in ASDs "has been well documented" and that "children who receive early intensive behavioral treatment have been shown to make substantial, sustained gains in IQ, language, academic performance, and adaptive behavior as well as some measures of social behavior."[34] ABA-based programs are now widely accepted and funded by most federal, state, and insurance payers.

---

34 SM Myers, CP Johnson; Council on Children with Disabilities (2007), "Management of children with autism spectrum disorders," *Pediatrics* 120, no.5 (2007): 1162–1182, doi:10.1542/peds.2007-2362.

CHAPTER 3

THE AUTISM SERVICES LANDSCAPE

When I made the decision in 2000 to collaborate with my colleague Bill and open Autism Spectrum Therapies (AST) in Los Angeles, California, there were a handful of large, established ABA service providers in the state, as well as a few smaller companies. There were also some individuals providing services that were not considered evidence-based. Given the existence of the state's Lanterman Act, the history of Lovaas at UCLA, the Koegels in Santa Barbara, and others—and the models for early intervention borne out of this research—autism services were not new to California.

At the time, service models mostly consisted of thirty- to forty-hour or more per week programs,

TOPICS AHEAD:

NOT ALL ABA IS CREATED EQUAL

TYPES OF SERVICES

CLINICAL PROGRAMS, CURRICULA, AND OUTCOMES

FUNDING SOURCES

A SOCIALLY CONSCIOUS BUSINESS OPPORTUNITY

delivered in-home and in-school, and funded by the state system, the regional center system, and school districts (in the case of school-age children). The typical clinical model was a Lovaas-style model with a rigid, structured methodology and clinical program. The focus was on providing intensive intervention directly to the child with little attention being paid to the needs of the family or toward designing programs within the context of the family system and dynamics.

FAQ:

WHAT IS THE LANTERMAN ACT?

The Lanterman Developmental Disabilities Act (Lanterman Act) of 1977 is a California Law that promises lifelong services and support to people with developmental disabilities. This law significantly expanded on the Lanterman Mental Retardation Act initially proposed in 1969. The law is designed to meet the needs and choices of the individual and declares that individuals with developmental disabilities have the same legal rights and responsibilities guaranteed to all others by federal and state laws and constitutions. To learn more about the history of Lanterman, refer to the further reading and information section.

The Lanterman Act establishes a system for advocacy and protection of these rights. State Assemblyman Frank D. Lanterman championed for the causes of individuals with disabilities throughout his career to ensure their civil rights and guarantee them the funds to support lifelong services.

Services are provided through state-operated developmental centers and community facilities, and contracts with twenty-one nonprofit regional centers throughout California. The regional centers serve as a local resource to help find and access the services and supports available to individuals with developmental disabilities and their families.

WHY IS CALIFORNIA SUCH A NEXUS OF SERVICES?

The Lanterman Act has resulted in a large and well-established funding system for autism services as well as other developmental disabilities and mental health issues. As a result, the provider network and system for service provision in California is five decades old and the autism service delivery model, as well as many others, is grounded and established.

My partner and I launched what was initially a boutique consulting company, recruiting a select group of masters- and doctoral-level professionals. Our initial goal when opening our doors was to provide consultation and training to school districts that were building capacity in classrooms, thereby enabling teachers to better manage the needs of individuals with autism. We also sought to provide specific social skills training programs to students within the context of their daily routines at school. Within a few months of working in some schools, we received requests to work with individual students and provide in-school and in-home support. We quickly grew from a small partnership with supervision meetings around my dining room table to a company recruiting highly skilled and educated clinicians from across the nation.

Our philosophy was one of deep collaboration with parents to focus our programs on the needs of the individual, taking into consideration their routines and specific needs, as well as the goals of the family. We also worked with funding sources to be as collaborative as possible and mitigate unnecessary stress and pressure wherever possible for all parties involved. Within months, our reputation started to grow as a company that could support families dealing with all kinds of challenging behavioral issues, that collaborated well with school districts and families, and that committed considerable resources to ensuring the quality of interventions and outcomes.

Shortly thereafter, our local regional center (one of the state funding agencies in California responsible for purchasing services on behalf of families) contacted us and requested that we develop a parent/primary caregiver-focused ABA program with a more naturalistic approach and methodology. The individuals at the regional center recognized that the current dominant programs were not generating the best outcomes and long-term prognoses and that the intensive, structured model was unrealistic for many families.

Our early in-home intervention program was evidence-based and rooted in the principles of ABA, yet was naturalistic and family-oriented. It focused on building functional communication, social, self-help, and play skills. The program included structured learning when appropriate and focused on naturalistic teaching strategies that parents and primary caregivers learned from working with interventionists and supervisors, so that parents and caregivers could use these strategies with their children when we were not present. Our philosophy was to create a living, breathing, child-directed, family-focused program that could exist 24/7 in a child's home; optimal outcomes are achieved with continued support and consistency. We emphasized the need for all caregivers to be involved in teaching and reinforcing newly acquired skills.

With the expansion of this program, we were providing services in the home for toddlers and positive behavioral support services for children in schools. When our toddlers turned three years old, they would enter a different federal and state funding environment, and our services expanded into additional types of school-funded, in-home, and school-based programs.

As a cofounder of AST, it was very important to me to bring my experience to this company and to strive to provide parents with the quality of services I would want for my own child, a quality I was not seeing much in the current provider landscape. As I reflected on the many different settings in which I had worked and the individuals with whom I had interacted, the values and mission of AST became clear for us.

My time in these academic and clinical environments formed the foundation of how I approach care and intervention: a naturalistic approach that utilizes ABA methodology and emphasizes the individual. It was this approach that made AST so successful. However, the market offers a variety of ABA-based services. It's important for investors to know that not all ABA is the same or will achieve the same results.

My experience has provided me with a unique look at the industry, and I believe there is much that we can do to improve the standards and outcomes. To do so, we must be willing to critically examine where we are today. In this chapter, I am going to detail how the services industry functions and what it looks like today. I'll share what I have learned from sitting down with individuals and stakeholders across the field, including insurance insiders, state funders, investors, legislators, parents, and the self-advocates who have gone through ABA intervention. I will highlight what we have done right and examine where there is still work to be done. I'll detail where services exist, their aims and approaches, and how socially conscious investors can help move the industry forward. We have to be able to question what we are doing and critically assess the outcomes. Who is benefiting? Who is not? And how can we improve?

NOT ALL ABA IS CREATED EQUAL

Nearly two decades since AST's inception, the field of autism services has changed quite significantly, some for the better and some not. While thousands of providers now exist across the nation, many hundreds of which are in California, the quality of ABA implementation and evidence-based intervention varies dramatically. While tens, perhaps hundreds, of thousands of families have access to services now, most families do not know how to differentiate between quality services, evidence-based practice, and services that do not offer "true" ABA.

FAQ:

WHAT ARE THE INDICATORS OF A QUALITY ABA PROGRAM?

The program is developed and supervised by a certified, credentialed individual. The individual overseeing the program must be a certified BCBA and ideally there should be other clinically licensed, credentialed, and experienced professionals in the organization providing oversight for the clinical model.

Programs are individualized to the needs of the individual based off the assessment. Cookie-cutter programs offering the same goals to each individual is a big red flag, as is simply "teaching to the deficits" in a cookie-cutter program, i.e. teaching only the skills missed on a specific assessment.

The goals are meaningful, functional, and build important skills for adulthood. The goals not only build on deficits, but address important strengths as well. A good question to ask is: If my child cannot do this skill when they are an adult, will someone else have to do it for them?

Data should be collected regularly and used to make decisions about program modifications. Data should be shared with the parent regularly.

The program is positive (not aversive or punishing) and includes many opportunities for positive reinforcement. The reinforcement is natural and preferred by the child.

The program is delivered in a manner that embeds generalization (the ability to perform the task or skill in multiple settings, with multiple people) and maintains skills that have been previously mastered.

Challenging behaviors are addressed and reduced in a behavior plan.

Parental involvement is mandatory. Parent and primary caregivers are a critical component of a good intervention plan and research has shown that outcomes are better for children whose parents participate in their intervention program.

When it comes to ABA, the question of intensity is a particularly big debate. The literature and research support the efficacy of a minimum of twenty-five hours of engagement per week for children in early intervention.[35] However, some companies—too many companies— use number of hours alone as the basis for recommending and providing intensive services. There are other variables to consider: the qualifications and experience of your staff; the training, continued supervision, and ongoing professional development of your staff; the fidelity of program implementation; the quality of data collection and degree to which programmatic decisions are based on actual progress and on the data; the clinical operations of the program; the degree to which programs are individualized for each client's needs;

---

35 National Research Council, *Educating Children with Autism,* (Washington D.C.: The National Academies Press, 2001).

and the experience and qualifications of those overseeing the clinical program.

· ·

What is a BCBA?

The board-certified behavior analyst (BCBA) is a graduate-level certification in behavior analysis. BCBAs are independent practitioners who provide behavior analytic services. They also supervise the work of board-certified assistant behavior analysts (BCaBA) and registered behavior technicians (RBT).

Requirements:

- Graduate degree from an accredited university

- Completion of acceptable graduate coursework in behavior analysis

- A defined period of supervised practical experience

- A passing grade on the BCBA exam

· ·

As was the case with our company, the quality of our services and the superior outcomes of our programs were due to the comprehensive nature of the consideration, attention, and resources devoted to each of these variables and more. Early on, we built a clinical team and think tank of sixteen highly qualified and experienced professionals (of whom nine held PhDs), from universities and research programs across the country, to continuously modify and update our clinical program and protocols to incorporate the latest research and evidence-based treatments. We were among the first to collaborate with universities to provide in-house training programs for BCBAs and grew our company early on to include over fifty BCBAs. Our company would scale to include over 750 employees serving over 1,500 families weekly in multiple states. Our training program for new employees was intensive, and employees had to demonstrate multiple levels of competency to advance in the company. Our employees were incredibly talented and passionate individuals who shared their gifts with our company and our families. Their alignment with our mission to make a meaningful difference in the lives of children was palpable, and many employees grew professionally with the organization for many years.

We were often condemned and vilified by parent advocacy groups and some of our competitors because we did not automatically recommend forty-plus hours for every child we evaluated. We were paying close attention to all the variables we considered critical to a superior ABA program, and we educated families on what questions to ask and how to measure success in an ABA program, whether we worked with them or not. We could demonstrate with data how well our clients were progressing, most often with fewer than forty hours a week. Today, many more companies are out there, some promoting highly intensive hours while foregoing adequate staff training, supervision, valid and reliable data collection, frequent program modification, customized programs, and adequate clinical oversight.

As our company grew to meet the demands of the growing needs for services, my role transformed multiple times, from clinician, supervisor, and coffeemaker to taking on the responsibilities of payroll, billing, human resources, and other activities in which, at inception, I had little experience. We experienced all the growing pains entrepreneurs go through when, as they say, you "build the plane while flying it." We grew administrative, clinical, and executive teams; learned to manage growth while working hard to maintain quality; and learned from our mistakes about the critical importance of pivoting, especially in a market like California. Ultimately, I assumed the true role of CEO, managing our executive team, who reported to our president and COO.

Providing services for individuals with autism is a rapidly growing field with increasing funding sources. Investors are becoming more attracted to the industry because of its revenue streams and incredible social importance. More autistic individuals have access to the services they need to help them than ever before. As the industry grows, even more people will have the opportunity to benefit from these services. But it is crucial that as the field grows, the quality of services continue to improve rather than stagnate or decline.

TYPES OF SERVICES

Autism services aim to provide support, learning, and the implementation of ABA to individuals living with autism. As every individual with autism is unique, these programs ought to be highly individualized. Depending on the age, needs, and circumstances of each individual and their family, services will vary. Other relevant variables are the types of funding available in their state or county, as well as the abundance or scarcity of service providers in their area. The focus of many of these services has been on early intervention due to legislation, funding, and research that supports the importance of capitalizing on early child development and brain growth during childhood, especially during the first five years.

Autism services include:
- In-home services

- Center-based services

- In-school services

- Community services
- Adult/Independent living services

IN-HOME SERVICES

In-home services comprise a large portion of the autism services field. This is intervention that takes place with a therapist or behavior interventionist in the home of the autistic individual. Recommendations for services range from fifteen to forty or more hours per week, every week. Some providers argue that to achieve the results demonstrated by Lovaas, services need to be intensive for all children: thirty-five to forty or more hours per week, five to seven days a week, every week. Without this level of consistency and intensity, limited progress will be made. Even for children with less intensive programs, consistency is key to progress.

In 2001, the U.S. Department of Education sponsored a study to examine appropriate services for young children (toddlers) with autism. The National Research Council published an extensive report after reviewing multiple programs and concluded that at a minimum, twenty-five hours per week, five days a week of intervention/educational engagement should be provided. However, for a variety of reasons, many children receive significantly fewer hours than that. The council concluded that educational services should begin as soon as a developmental delay (autism) is suspected and that programming should consist of "systematically planned and developmentally appropriate educational activities" that are designed toward defined and measured goals and objectives.[36] The report describes that programs' contents should vary based on the age, developmental level, strengths, challenges of the child, and the family's needs. This

---

36 Ibid.

speaks to the importance of individualized programs that evolve and change as children grow and both their needs and the needs of their family change.

Once a behavioral services provider receives a referral for in-home services, an in-home assessment is conducted by a supervisor, hopefully with BCBA credentials and some experience managing autism programs and working with families. I say "hopefully" because while this should be the standard for service delivery, it is not, and this is one of the factors contributing to the decrease in quality and adherence to the science of our field. The in-home assessment is designed to evaluate the environment and the needs of the child and their family and should include direct observation of the child in their natural environment, interviews with the parents, a functional behavior assessment (FBA), and the administration of appropriate standardized measures to assess adaptive functioning, communication, and other functional skills. Once the assessment has been conducted and a program (ideally an individualized one, not a cookie-cutter version) has been developed, the provider will then recommend a certain number of weekly hours during which the child would receive behavior intervention. If approved by the funding source, services begin, with an interventionist visiting the home, often daily, to provide services. In my experience, services typically involve two to four hours per day of intervention, with some funding sources approving more intensive programs that approach the recommended guidelines for an appropriately intensive early intervention program. The number of hours approved varies dramatically across providers, even within the same city.

What set our company apart in the early 2000s was our naturalistic, family-focused approach. While this approach was being taught at universities and in clinics, it was not a standard practice in community-based programs at the time. We emphasized the need to include parents and caregivers in our interventions and collected data on caregiver participation in sessions. Many companies will recommend forty hours or more per week of intervention, regardless of the needs of the child and the capacity of the family. But by giving parents and caregivers the strategies and tools they need to continue intervention on their own, the number of hours a therapist needed to be present in the home was reduced. This establishes a consistent system of contingencies and reinforcement that continues twenty-four hours a day, seven days a week.

Good intervention approaches should be focused foremost on the skills children need to function independently, care for themselves, and build independent lives; such as learning to groom and bathe themselves, safety, social skills, academic skills, as well as long-term goals that support independence as an adult. It's important that intervention prioritizes practical and necessary skills. As we touched upon in the last chapter, much consideration is required when determining what each child should focus on learning. The goal is to build toward a future for that individual, not follow a prescribed program that may not fit this person's needs or abilities.

IN-SCHOOL SERVICES

The goal of services in the school is to aid children in their ability to learn and interact within the school environment and to build capacity within classrooms for children with special needs to participate. Due to IDEA, which defines the requirements of "least restrictive environments," many children with diagnoses of learning disabilities and developmental disorders are placed in general education classrooms because the goal is for them to spend as much time as possible with peers who do not require special education. The teachers in general education classrooms often need education and guidance to create the best learning environment for the spectrum of learning needs and accommodations required by children with differing learning challenges.

. . . .

The Individuals with Disabilities Education Act (IDEA) is a federal law ensuring services to children with disabilities throughout the nation, making a free and appropriate public education available to eligible children with disabilities and ensuring special education and related services to those children.

IDEA governs how states and public agencies provide early intervention, special education, and related services to more than 6.5 million eligible infants, toddlers, children, and youth with disabilities.

Infants and toddlers with disabilities (birth to age two), and their families, receive early intervention services under IDEA Part C.

Children and youth (ages three to twenty-two) receive special education and related services under IDEA Part B.

LRE:

Under IDEA, least restrictive environment (LRE) means that a student who has a disability should have the opportunity to be educated with non-disabled peers, to the greatest extent appropriate.

. . . .

Services for autistic children at school are generally comprised of workshops, group or individual classroom consultations, teacher training, and one-on-one shadowing of students in the classroom. Teacher training and group workshops are geared toward providing autism education to teachers and staff, so they have a better understanding of the needs of their individual students affected by autism and other disabilities. Other consultations can focus on providing support for the school administration and are designed to help schools offer more support for students with special needs as a whole, as well as build capacity in their classrooms. Teacher training focuses on training educators in some basics of ABA and strategies to manage behavioral challenges so they can more effectively communicate with and teach autistic students. There are a growing number of schools leading the way in this regard, but sadly the majority of schools do not currently offer adequate support for autistic students.

Companies also train and supply "shadows" (one-to-one aides) for students with autism. A shadow accompanies a child with autism for part or all of their day at school and helps them function and participate in classroom and school activities. This structure provides a one-on-one "tutor" who understands how to work with children with autism, which minimizes the demand on teachers. Shadows are able to help children navigate their schedules, transition to the next class, and participate in a meaningful way. Shadows work on specific goals throughout the day and throughout each lesson, such as helping a child with following teacher instructions, and providing prompts when necessary. Prompts can be verbal ("Jack, the teacher asked you to take out your notebook") or visual (prompting the student to check their visual schedule or look at a picture that provides a reminder of what activity is occurring in the classroom).

While only some states have programs at school or in classrooms geared specifically toward children with autism, all states are required to provide funding for support and individualized education due to federal mandates in IDEA. If a student qualifies for IDEA, they'll receive something called an individualized education plan (IEP).

Rather than following the general education curriculum for that grade, the student will follow their own individualized curriculum that is geared toward their special needs. Parents and the school meet and develop goals for the year, which serve as a basis for the individualized curriculum.

. . . .

What is FAPE?

FAPE is the right to a free and appropriate education. All qualified persons with disabilities within the jurisdiction of a school district are entitled to FAPE.

Section 504 of the Rehabilitation Act of 1973 protects the rights of individuals with disabilities in programs and activities that receive federal financial assistance, including federal funds. Section 504 provides that "No otherwise qualified individual with a disability in the United States ... shall, solely by reason of her or his disability, be excluded from the participation in, be denied the benefits of, or be subjected to discrimination under any program or activity receiving Federal financial assistance ... "

The Section 504 regulation requires a school district to provide a "free appropriate public education" (FAPE) to each qualified person with a disability who is in the school district's jurisdiction, regardless of the nature or severity of the person's disability.[37]

. . . .

This is a very important area of autism services because, while many schools have no one on staff who has been educated on autism or

---

37 U.S. Department of Education, Office for Civil Rights, Free Appropriate Public Education for Students With Disabilities: Requirements Under Section 504 of the Rehabilitation Act of 1973, Washington, D.C., 2010.

how to work with children with autism, educators are faced with teaching children with autism every day. Schools are increasingly realizing their limitations in terms of expertise and ability to offer appropriate support. This is a largely unfilled space that presents incredible opportunity for the autism services industry.

CENTER-BASED SERVICES

While there is significant research and many arguments to support the efficacy of intervention in the natural environment (generally the home), for some individuals and families, home-based services are not an option. The type of services made accessible to families may depend on their funding source or geographical location. Others argue that center-based services offer benefits that are not available in home-based models and that they offer children better outcomes.[38] Some state and commercial funding sources prefer to see a child receive at least a portion of their services in their natural environment, which for a very young child, under the age of three, is typically the home.

Service providers whose therapists are driving to clients' homes daily to provide in-home services require operating strategies that account for all the variables that accompany managing and scaling a distributed workforce. Without a service strategy and critical aspects of service delivery—such as supervision and training of staff, program management, and back-office processes—the quality of services will be affected. For those offering a center-based approach, operating

---

38 J Roberts, K Williams, M Carter et al., "A randomised controlled trial of two early intervention programs for young children with autism: centre-based with parent program and home-based," *Research in Autism Spectrum Disorders* 5, no. 4 (2011): 1553–1566; Dennis R. Dixon, Claire O. Burns, Doreen Granpeesheh et al., "A Program Evaluation of Home and Center-Based Treatment for Autism Spectrum Disorder," *Behav Anal Pract* 10, no. 3 (September 2017): 307–312.

costs are different (often lower, depending on real estate costs), there is less complexity, and the operators can exert much more control over the therapeutic environment, including utilization of staff, program and staff supervision, and ongoing training of staff.

Many center-based programs promote their services as a preferred mode of delivery by emphasizing that they can minimize distractions, restrict access to preferred toys (make the toys only accessible during intervention, whereas parents may give them to the child at home and cause the toys to lose their "appeal" during intervention), and enable parents to take on other duties, such as care of other children or parents, during intervention. However, many of the center-based programs I have reviewed do not require much parent involvement, which has implications for generalization of skills and adaptability in the home environment.

Research has detailed the pros and cons of both environments. A review of randomized, controlled trials examining the outcomes of parent-mediated early intervention for young children with autism demonstrated that when parents were involved in intervention and received training, the way they interacted with their children changed as intended. In addition, improved outcomes for the children were demonstrated, such as improved understanding of language and communication skills and a decrease in the severity of autism characteristics.[39] Other research has found that children make more gains from center-based intervention (with and without parent training) than home-based. However, there were considerable factors in each of these studies, such as intensity of treatment differing between the

---

39 IP Oono, EJ Honey, and H McConachie, "Parent-mediated early intervention for young children with autism spectrum disorders (ASD)," *Cochrane Database Syst Rev,* (2013), doi:10.1002/14651858.CD009774.pub2.

two groups being compared, that indicate more research is needed before drawing conclusions.[40]

Many young adults who experienced the more rigid, less naturalistic version of ABA as children shared with me their aversion to being made to sit in a small clinic room for hours. A couple of them have become aides at schools or direct interventionists working in ABA companies, and they tend toward modalities where they can move around, go into different rooms during intervention, and go outside. "Learning by doing" is how they see effective ABA.

While center-based services may be a good fit for some, intervention should still be individualized and should use the child's natural inclinations and interests as motivators. Goals should be set not in terms of normalization but to improve communication and the child's ability to function and interact with their environment.

ADULT/INDEPENDENT LIVING SERVICES

While a large segment of the autism services industry is geared toward children and early intervention, there are a myriad of services that can be provided for adults with autism, as well. These services range from limited and basic support roles for individuals who may require minimal help (a weekly check-in) in their day-to-day lives to directly caring for individuals with intensive needs who are entirely dependent on others for their ongoing care and support. Those who require support may live at home with their parents or may live in a

---

40   J Roberts, K Williams, M Carter et al., "A randomised controlled trial of two early intervention programs for young children with autism: centre-based with parent program and home-based," *Research in Autism Spectrum Disorders* 5, no. 4 (2011): 1553–1566; Dennis R. Dixon, Claire O. Burns, Doreen Granpeesheh et al., "A Program Evaluation of Home and Center-Based Treatment for Autism Spectrum Disorder," *Behav Anal Pract* 10, no. 3 (September 2017): 307-312.

group home, an apartment, or another residential environment with other individuals who function at a similar level.

Group homes are homes within the community, owned and staffed twenty-four hours a day by a service provider, and typically house four to eight residents. The primary goal of group homes is intended to be the promotion of independent skills such as meal preparation, money management, home maintenance, cleaning, laundry, hygiene, and so on. They also offer activities such as going out to lunch, seeing a movie, taking a walk, or arts and crafts. These are services that can get individuals out of the group home and engaged in enjoyable activities in the community. Some offer vocational training or daily transportation to day programs offering training or other activities.

In reality, many group home environments are built to serve the group and not the individual. While this has been necessary for many individuals and is sometimes the only option, it's an environment that doesn't offer a lot of choice or self-determination. There's usually a regimented or very limited schedule of activities and prescribed meals. I have not visited many group homes where clients could make their own food whenever they wanted and choose whatever they wanted to eat, for example.

For individuals who are more independent, living with one or two roommates in an apartment is often an option. For these adults who can manage many of their own needs but may need some assistance or someone to check in on them for safety, supported living services is a good option. Perhaps these roommates can cook but need some support in meal planning. They might need help figuring out transportation to work or learning how to clean their apartment or do laundry. Supported living services programs are directed by the consumer, not the program, and there is much more emphasis on community integration. In these instances, having someone check in or stay overnight could be beneficial. Every individual is unique, so services have to be customizable.

For adults who need more supervision than that offered by supported living but don't require the level of support provided in a group home, supervised living is an option. This is another residential model, where adults may live in homes or apartments with one or two roommates. Staff support is available around the clock, if needed, but the staff member does not live in the home with the autistic adults. Staff may provide additional supports such as assistance with planning meals and daily schedules, as well as direct instruction and support.

Many higher-functioning individuals reside at home with their parents. While this may be suitable for them in the short-term, this limited solution provides difficult complications. At some point, these individuals' parents will no longer be able to care for them, and if they have not learned the skills they need to live independently, or if they have not had exposure to alternate living situations, they will have limited options and a difficult transition. Programs focused on developing independent living skills are needed to prepare them for the day when they will have to make that transition—a transition that is better the sooner it is made, as the longer individuals live with their parents or family members, the harder it is for them to leave.

There are new and innovative residential and nonresidential programs and communities being established for autistic adults that offer the opportunity to develop independent living skills and social skills in addition to practical and employment skills that will help these young adults transition toward employment, higher education, and independence. Other programs offer long-term living options with support and daily activities and work. These communities and programs are being established on farms, vineyards, and ranches and incorporate work skills classes and vocational training in the areas of farming, agriculture, and craftwork, as well as the management of cafes, bookstores, coffee shops, and other microbusinesses. Others offer more urban locations where participants live on-site and are able to attend college or work in the community, with the goal of moving on to independent living and employment.

Adults with autism can also utilize day programs, which offer structured daily activities, supportive therapies, and opportunities for skill building. These usually involve a mix of training and leisure. There are center-based and community-based day programs that work to integrate adults into their local communities and individualize programs to help each adult learn the skills they want to learn. As with any other type of program, there are some great and innovative day programs teaching great skills, and there are others which resemble daycares.

COMMUNITY-BASED SERVICES

What really gives someone independence? What gives them a sense of personal agency? What gives a person these things is the ability to choose. Choice empowers people by giving them control over their lives. Community-based services can help individuals with disabilities gain independence by imparting the skills they need to make choices.

Currently, the application of our methodology and many of its programs are failing in this regard. Education and interventions need to be more comprehensive; we need to teach autistic individuals how to live in a choice-driven world and how to have meaningful participation in their communities.

In 2014, new federal regulations were published by the Centers for Medicare and Medicaid Services (CMS) for home- and community-based services (HCBS). These new rules require homes and programs where HCBS are delivered to meet specific criteria in order to qualify for federal funding under Medicaid (called Medi-Cal in California). Each state must write a plan for how its HCBS programs meet these new rules. States have until March 17, 2022 to implement the requirements for home- and community-based settings in accordance with CMS-approved plans.

HCBS are long-term services and support provided in home- and community-based settings. These services can include both medical services and nonmedical services. Standard services can include, but are not limited to, case management (i.e., support and service coordination), homemaking, a home health aide, personal care, adult day health services, habilitation (both day and residential), and respite care.

The intention of this new ruling is to ensure that home- and community-based settings are exactly that: places representing what it is like to live in a home and community, rather than a setting that is institutional or restrictive in nature. The implications of these new regulations will be significant for some programs, which will require substantial adjustments to meet these new requirements. For example, the regulations require that individuals be able to make life choices, including those of daily activities, physical environment, living situation, and with whom they spend their time. In addition, individuals must have the freedom to choose when and what to eat, welcome visitors at any time, and control their own schedules. States can also propose other types of services that may assist in diverting and/or transitioning individuals from institutional settings into their homes and community.

CLINICAL PROGRAMS, CURRICULA, AND OUTCOMES

At the heart of any autism service provider is its clinical program and the curricula used to build that program. There are good curricula in autism service and ABA intervention. Some companies put out curricula that are comprehensive, extensive, and beneficial to follow. However, some curricula are too narrow or rote, placing too much emphasis on linear learning rather than necessary, age-appropriate and functional skills. Other times, the curriculum is well designed, but the application is too cookie-cutter and not individualized properly.

As we've discussed, it's crucial to adapt and customize interventions based on the individual's needs and interests. For example, I have read assessment reports where the child only ate two foods or could not tolerate drinking water. Then, upon examination of the program, there were no goals geared toward feeding, food selectivity, or helping the child consume water. The program was entirely based on an unestablished (not evidence-based), off-the-shelf curriculum. The child's pressing needs should take priority, but often they do not. While some of these off-the-shelf curricula have data to support them (others have none), they aren't designed or being used in a way that enables providers to customize and individualize the material. Individualization of programming is key.

Every individual has unique needs, which interventions and services should address, and unique strengths, which interventions should build upon. Programs need to be less linear, less rigid, and more fluid. They need to be adaptable and customizable to address whatever specific needs and goals a child has. Not every child is going to need the exact same skills to maximize opportunities and potential in adulthood.

THE IMPORTANCE OF OUTCOMES

As we touched upon briefly in the last chapter, service providers have generally done a poor job of properly assessing the outcomes of their programs. The nature of the disorder makes this very challenging, because every child starts at a different point. Each child is unique; you simply cannot directly compare one to another. Conducting outcome research when providing services in the home adds additional complexities, but it is possible and necessary. The word *analysis* in "applied behavior analysis" emphasizes the fact that we are supposed to be using the data we collect to demonstrate that our intervention is responsible for the change in behavior or the skill acquisition and that further programmatic modifications should be based on that analysis.

Data are typically collected on an individual basis, looking at one client at a time, comparing their performance on tasks and behaviors at baseline (before intervention started) against various points throughout intervention. This is called *single-subject research design* and produces quantifiable data; a child may have had an average of twelve aggressive episodes a day, but now—after behavior reduction techniques and the teaching of functional communication—is displaying between zero and two tantrums per day. Thus, scientific, empirical data can be collected to validate the methodology. This is the only way to really gauge your intervention; the science allows for an objective measure of outcomes.

In group design research, two groups of randomly assigned subjects—an experimental group that receives an intervention, and a control group that does not receive the intervention—are compared to each other to determine if the intervention was responsible for the change in behavior or skills acquisition. This type of research, the randomized control trial (RCT), is a high standard of research design, because it aims to remove as many sources of bias as possible from the process. The randomization of subjects to the two different groups and the participation of only one group in the intervention, are both designed to control as many external variables as possible. Some of the most widely used clinical programs for autism today have not been evaluated using the RCT process. Despite this lack of scientifically validated efficacy and clinical utility, companies and investors are choosing to build potentially large platforms of services on these clinical programs.

Outcome data are very important, because that is the only way to demonstrate progress. But the industry has a problem when it comes to consistency. If there is no consistency between companies on how data are collected and outcomes are assessed, then any data derived are useless on a scale beyond that business. The goal should be for providers to be able to demonstrate the efficacy and clinical utility of their programs internally by measuring outcomes for their participants, as well as be able to compare data with competitors to develop industry standards for measuring outcomes of behavioral interventions. This does not require sharing proprietary strategic initiatives or intellectual property; it only requires sharing measurement methodologies and data.

The inconsistencies within the service provider market are also internal. I've looked at companies that use one assessment measure at baseline, a different measure six months later, and sometimes a third measure at twelve months. It's illogical and irresponsible, as it does not provide a standard, objective measure of progress over time. Just because you can anecdotally observe a child and say he or she has made progress does not mean you can attribute it to intervention, and it certainly cannot be quantified accurately if there is no consistency in measures or assessments.

Precise, generalizable data are also important when it comes to funding sources. Whether the sources are state funds or private insurance companies, they will be looking for outcomes that are both consistent and measurable. Further, these sources may move toward performance-based reimbursement. As the industry grows, providers and investors genuinely need to look closely at this and develop some standards for the industry as a whole. We should be able to compare one provider to another, which is not currently possible, because everyone is using different measures and, as we discussed earlier, there is a protective, proprietary attitude where few are willing to share their data or even measure the same outcomes.

THERAPEUTIC GOALS

Just as individualized, flexible programs are optimal, there needs to be individualized benchmarks for progress. Intervention is currently based on the chronological age of a child versus the age level at which the child is performing or communicating. So, a child may be six years old but is only communicating at a three-year-old level. Intervention aims to close this gap. While this is an important measure, we have to avoid approaches geared solely toward normalization. Teaching differentiation of colors at the elementary school level is appropriate. However, focusing on colors at fifteen years old, at the expense of teaching vocational skills and independent living skills, will negatively affect the quality of that child's life as an adult. Some individuals will never be indistinguishable from their neurotypical peers.

The question to ask is, "If this child does not learn this skill, will someone else have to do it for them?" The real benchmarks of success are not intervention hours per week, or even short-term acquisition of skills; they are quality of life and improved life skills that are meaningful in the long-term and improve one's ability to live as independent a life as possible in adulthood.

Standardizing short-term outcomes is critical for the industry to evolve, but it doesn't stop there. It's important to track both short-term and long-term outcomes for individuals. That means understanding how a child has progressed after one day of services, after six months, and then following their entire program. We also need to look at how the industry is performing and what the costs and utilization of services look like. These are critical aspects of steering the industry in the right direction and ensuring that all families have access to services. In the next two chapters I will share insights from autistic individuals and from statistics demonstrating that these outcomes are significantly inadequate.

FAQ:

WHAT GOALS SHOULD A GOOD ABA PROGRAM INCLUDE?

The most important element of an intervention program is that it is personalized according to the needs of the individual. These needs are informed by observation of the individual, standardized assessments, interviews with parents and primary caregivers, and a functional behavior assessment (FBA) if necessary to assess the function of any challenging behaviors. The program should take place in the natural environment (as much as possible), be delivered by trained professionals, and be family-focused, meaning the family is involved in determining what is important to them and the participant.

Goals should include:

- Increasing selected functional behaviors

- Teaching new functional skills (including communication, social, and adaptive)

- Maintaining selected behaviors

- Reducing interfering or challenging behaviors

- Teaching functional replacement behaviors

- Generalizing behaviors (this is embedded into the programming)

- Increasing parental skills and incorporating parental participation into all aspects of the program

- Collecting daily data to track progress and inform programmatic modifications and progression of goals. Re-assessment of skills using the same standardized measures should be occurring at regular intervals to assess progress.

FUNDING SOURCES

The autism services industry is dependent on third-party payers, meaning that services providers have customers who pay for the services (the funding source) and clients who consume the services but are most often not the people paying for them. Payment for these services typically comes from multiple sources including school districts (as mandated by federal law), government sources (such as Medicaid), state sources (typically your local state agency supporting individuals with developmental disabilities), TRICARE (government managed health insurance for the military), or private insurance companies. Funding is addressed in more detail in chapter 4. Fortunately for individuals and families living with autism, more funding is becoming available, which means greater access to much-needed services.

The good news is that over the past decade, many more states have legislated specific autism mandates requiring certain insurers to provide autism services. The introduction of this new funding stream into the market has increased access to services for many thousands of families and has also increased investor interest

The question to ask is, "If this child does not learn this skill, will someone else have to do it for them?" The real benchmarks of success are not intervention hours per week, or even short-term acquisition of skills; they are quality of life and improved life skills that are meaningful in the long-term and improve one's ability to live as independent a life as possible in adulthood.

in the sector. In addition, insurance generally funds more intensive service hours than many state agency contracts do, so families have access to more care than they previously had. However, there is still a lot of room for improvement in this area.

Generally, private insurance companies would rather have one contract with a larger provider that can serve many children across state lines than hold fifty contracts with smaller providers. That means there is a market for providers to grow and become substantial players, and there is logic to the consolidation of the market to create larger platforms that can serve and maintain these types of funding relationships. The problem is that for smaller companies and startups, cutting into that pie may be initially challenging, and scaling a company with the administrative burden that accompanies some of these funding streams often proves difficult. One of the best ways to differentiate your company is to have a service model with objective, clear outcome measures, as these are what insurance companies are looking for.

Once an individual receives a diagnosis of autism, the insurance provider will authorize a functional assessment to determine service need. Upon completion of the assessment, service providers make recommendations as to the intensity and goals of the program. The number of weekly hours is based on the assessment of need, the age of the child, and other factors, such as family availability for intervention. As discussed previously, these recommendations can range from fewer than ten hours up to more than forty hours per week. Funding sources will often limit the number of hours they approve regardless of age or need for services. I have seen many programs where the recommendation was for twenty-five hours per week of intervention, but the funding source only approved ten hours per week.

Providers are also often caught between recommending the hours they believe are appropriate and not being able to staff those hours, or families not being available for the hours funded. Providers can negatively affect their reputation by repeatedly recommending hours when they don't have the necessary resources to provide that many hours, even if the recommendations are clinically appropriate. The utilization of contracted hours is an important variable in the clinical operations of a behavioral service company.

FAQ:
___

HOW IS MEDICAL NECESSITY ESTABLISHED FOR ABA SERVICES WITH COMMERCIAL INSURANCE?

There is no standard across the autism services industry that determines medical necessity (MNC) or level of care guidelines (LOC) for treatment. Medical necessity criteria can vary greatly from one organization to another and they do not provide interpretations for appropriate levels of care.

ABA is still widely misunderstood by many insurance companies. This, coupled with the lack of consistency and quality of care within the ABA provider community, makes it more challenging for insurance management teams to review and evaluate programs and treatment recommendations. The lack of collaboration between providers in the ABA community adds to these issues.

To determine MNC, a diagnosis of autism spectrum disorder (ASD) is required, usually provided by a licensed clinical psychologist, pediatric neurologist, or developmental pediatrician using validated assessment tools.

Once a diagnosis has been received, a credentialed service provider will conduct an observation of the individual, a developmental assessment using a validated tool, and a functional behavior assessment (FBA) to gather information about problem behaviors. The information gathered from these assessments inform the design of the individualized treatment plan.

The determination that the individual's ability to function and participate at an age-appropriate level is prevented by behavioral excesses (i.e. potential for self-harm or safety concerns) and the absence of functional skills (i.e. communication, social skills, or self-care) is generally what forms the basis for a determination of medical necessity for intervention.

Funding sources have generally similar core requirements and definitions regarding deficits in functioning and impairments in skills that determine eligibility. Funding sources vary substantially in terms of what kinds of programs are funded, how hours are authorized, the reporting requirements, etc.

There are several considerations that factor into a medical necessity decision, a few of which are:

- The contract and benefit design of the member's insurance plan dictate which medical necessity criteria are applicable

- The willingness of family members to participate in program

- An environment where the participant can learn and partake in the program

- The manner in which program goals are written and the appropriateness of goals

- The goals of the treatment plan are specific, quantifiable, measurable, and relate to developmental deficits

- The medical stability of the individual (does not require hospitalization or other forms of medical care that prevent participation)

A SOCIALLY CONSCIOUS BUSINESS OPPORTUNITY

The industry is growing, and that growth will ensure greater access. But much work needs to be done to ensure that growth coincides with improvement in the quality of services and long-term outcomes. More capital will be needed to allow companies the resources they need to do so effectively.

As someone who deeply cares about helping individuals, the idea of selling investors and providers on the industry is sometimes tricky, as investor interests can occasionally conflict with putting the client's needs first. But an enterprise that is not profitable is one that will not be around long. It is important to balance the integrity of quality clinical interventions with the necessary business practices to help this industry grow and provide services to more and more individuals who need them. If we want adequate resources made available for those who need them, investors are necessary. Thus, it is important to demonstrate how and why the autism services industry is a good investment, particularly for those investors who are looking to make a social impact as well as a return on their investment.

I want to emphasize, however, just how remarkable this opportunity is, not just because of the profit potential but because it addresses a global need and transforms lives. This is a tremendous opportunity for socially conscious companies and investors to truly make a difference. It's a natural fit for behavioral healthcare companies that are already geared toward helping people, and for entrepreneurs who want to make the world a better place.

More investment will create more trained professionals and increase the number of service providers. More providers will be able to help more individuals and better prepare more schools to work with children with autism. Additional resources and the support of sophisticated business minds will enable clinicians to focus on outcomes and standardizing measures across the industry, while investors support the management of back-office administration, operations, infrastructure, strategic growth plans, and progressive public policy changes. I believe the pressure of a larger investment community will force this industry to professionalize and compete in a more productive manner. Greater capital investment can change the entire landscape for individuals living with autism and their families.

We can tap into the awesome power of markets and use it to further this cause. We can offer quality services with heart and compassion while also generating the capital needed to help others. Together, investors and providers can create an industry that is both profitable and transformative—one that provides jobs and helps a segment of the population that has been badly neglected. Together, we can work to evolve the industry, to make the necessary changes and additions that will achieve the best outcomes for autistic individuals as they go on to live independent lives.

CHAPTER 4

STRENGTHS AND SHORTFALLS OF THE ABA INDUSTRY

A BA-related services are a quickly growing market helping millions of individuals in a multitude of capacities. ABA's most valuable successes have been in helping autistic individuals make connections regarding language and the use of communication, develop social skills, reduce maladaptive behaviors, better understand their emotions, and navigate their environments. These services have been transformational for many individuals, helping them achieve long-term success and allowing them to better interact with the world at large. It has enabled many

TOPICS AHEAD:

WHERE THE ABA INDUSTRY NEEDS IMPROVEMENT

THE IMPACT OF FUNDING

WHAT'S MISSING FROM OUTCOMES?

EMPLOYMENT AND SOCIAL ACTIVITY

HEALTH

LIVING SITUATION AND INDEPENDENCE

RELATIONSHIPS

WHAT'S AT STAKE?

young individuals to live at home with their families and attend school. The value of these benefits for individuals on the spectrum is incalculable, and today there is an opportunity for the ABA industry to double down on its strengths and overcome its shortfalls.

One individual with whom I spoke, Christine, credits ABA with significantly improving her life and giving her many of the skills she needs to succeed in the world. After many experiences with different ABA therapists who were not attuned to her needs or way of processing the world, Christine credits her most recent ABA therapist with making a real difference in her life. She treated Christine like an equal and put effort into making a personal connection with her. During adolescence, one of the most challenging periods of development for all children, Christine's therapist helped her navigate her emotions by giving her a visual tool to understand her feelings and moods.

"It helped me manage my emotions and to a point I was able to identify how I was feeling and what strategy I could use and [what] alternative behaviors [I could use] without fixing them [my feelings]. I think I would not have been able to go to college if I didn't get into [ABA] therapy. It taught me self-advocacy and self-awareness."

Christine's story highlights just how beneficial ABA intervention and a compassionate approach can be and drives home the valuable service the professionals who provide ABA are performing. However, despite the gains Christine made in many areas of academic and adaptive functioning, she experiences social isolation, and is still working towards greater independence and social integration.

Others have shared with me the aversive nature of DTT and being forced to sit and repeat trial after trial of a specific skill. One young man shared with me how, because he could not respond correctly in a verbal manner as a young child, he was exposed repeatedly to the same tasks—naming colors, shapes, and objects—while in his head he was performing math calculations. He simply could not express himself until he was older.

Stories such as his underscore the gaps in the provider industry, which will continue to widen as a generation of autistic individuals become adults and will be unable to continue relying on aging parents and caregivers. Current and future providers and industry professionals will need to address some of the lingering deficits of many ABA efforts, the lack of standardized outcome measures, and the long-term shortsightedness of the practice to ensure that autistic individuals are given the best tools possible to live fully functional, meaningful, and self-determined lives.

After working in the industry for decades and speaking daily with service providers and those with autism and their families, it's clear that as an industry, we have to keep looking to the future. The autism services industry, like any business or science-based field, demands constant refinement, progress, and evolution. To look forward, we must not be afraid to take a critical look at current practices and methods. Only by doing this can we determine where we should be heading.

The transition from the institutionalization of individuals with developmental disabilities such as autism in past decades to a population living in our communities has been a tremendously positive move. However, this transition also presents new challenges. ASD is estimated to affect more than three million individuals in the United States alone. We are facing an urgent situation where an aging and growing population of individuals will no longer have adequate living situations or the skills needed to make it on their own. As an industry, we need to recognize this and start acting to address it.

FAQ:

HOW ARE ELIGIBILITY CRITERIA DETERMINED FOR RECEIPT OF SERVICES?

Eligibility criteria for receipt of services vary by funding source and by state.

A diagnosis of autism spectrum disorder is required to be eligible for services.

Generally, a behavioral assessment is conducted to determine deficits in developmentally appropriate self-care and independent living skills, social communicative skills, and behavioral and safety concerns.

The exact eligibility criteria, as well as the types of services, number of authorized hours, and format of intervention vary by funding source.

IS ACUITY OF AUTISM A FACTOR IN RECEIVING SERVICES?

Acuity of autism is a factor in that the degree to which impairment of skills and deficits in functioning impact the individual's life determines the type and intensity of the program and services.

The turning point is twofold: not only is a population of adults struggling to integrate into the community, but currently one in sixty-eight children are diagnosed with the disorder, making it one of the fastest-growing and most prominent developmental disorders globally. These individuals are not automatically developing dynamic thinking and intelligence—skills they will need to navigate the world. Many are not learning the fundamental social interaction and relational skills needed to maintain a job or develop long-lasting relationships.

In the previous chapters, we established that the research and application of ABA created a scientifically proven body of interventions that have had positive, life-changing effects on many thousands of people. In this chapter, I explore an assessment of current ABA model deficits, present a proactive approach to better facilitate funding, and examine long-term service outcomes. I will also analyze statistics to gain a clear picture of what is being done well and what must happen so the industry can improve.

WHERE THE ABA INDUSTRY NEEDS IMPROVEMENT

Christine's story at the beginning of the chapter demonstrates just how impactful ABA can be. With the appropriate support at school, Christine attended and graduated college. She is employed and holds a board position advocating for individuals like her. However, despite her participation in multiple ABA programs, Christine feels she has not acquired the tools she needs to live a completely independent life and forge the kind of personal relationships she desires. She believes had she received better programming as a child and teenager that she'd be further ahead as an adult. Her story exemplifies the strengths and shortfalls of current ABA applications. It's important that we recognize just how valuable ABA is and what it has done for people's lives. We must, however, acknowledge that there are deficits in many service delivery programs, including poor clinical quality and the use of unestablished interventions; a rigid structure; a lack of programmatic emphasis on functionality; lack of emphasis on the development of dynamic thinking, relationship development, and future independence; limited training of professionals (direct interventionists and program supervisors); poor data collection; poor documentation; and a disregard for educating the general public.

FAQ:

WHY IS ABA THE TREATMENT OF CHOICE/THE MOST WIDELY FUNDED TREATMENT?

Applied behavior analysis is an empirically validated methodology that applies the principles of human behavior to a wide variety of settings (home, school, the community, etc.) to diminish behavioral excesses and teach the skills necessary for communication, social interaction, and adaptive functioning.

ABA has a very extensive body of research to support its efficacy and clinical utility. Many scientifically valid behavioral interventions have been developed based on the principles of ABA, and together these interventions can address a vast array of behavioral and safety concerns as well as skills critical to daily functioning and learning.

First, most of the current ABA providers use programs that focus on teaching skills but fail to emphasize functionality and relationship development. They fail to view the child they are working with as the adult they will become. I interviewed three state funding representatives for autism services who review the clinical program designs for hundreds of ABA companies across three U.S. states, including California, as well as the individual client programs, assessments and progress reports for thousands of children in these states. A major theme from those discussions was that many ABA providers today are effectively using off-the-shelf clinical ABA programs without any customization of programs for individual children. This cookie-cutter approach undermines the effectiveness of ABA, because every child with autism has unique challenges and strengths, and individualization will produce the best results.

Another theme was the lack of development of personal relationships and rapport between therapist and client. Interestingly, one of the chief complaints I hear about ABA intervention from adults today is how impersonal it felt and how the therapist failed to connect with them as a person. In addition, many providers within these organizations are not educated in child development and have little to no understanding of family systems. Providers cannot assist a person in learning to function in a social world if the providers themselves do not understand the social world. There is little emphasis on teaching the social-emotional aspects of relating to people or environments.

In more recent years, with the massive demand for autism services, we have seen the development of credentialing programs that focus specifically on training professionals (BCBAs, RBTs [registered behavior technicians], etc.) in ABA for autism. As a result, there are professionals in the community who understand autism and ABA but have not experienced a full breadth of experience in a variety of settings with a range of age groups and types of disorders. In addition, many of these new certification programs do not provide a foundation in family systems or understanding autism within the family ecosystem.

For example, you can obtain a certificate in behavior analysis, or an online master's degree along with your BCBA certification, by taking online coursework that is entirely focused on ABA, disabilities, and intervention. I researched a number of these programs offered by various universities across the country. While these programs meet the requirements of the Behavior Analyst Certification Board, out of the thirty to thirty-four hours of required coursework for a master's degree, only three hours were devoted to a general child development course. None of the programs I reviewed required coursework in family systems, counseling skills, or lifespan development—all critical skills and knowledge when working with families and planning futures for individuals, regardless of their special needs. When I discussed this with a colleague recently, she commented that getting BCBA certified today demonstrates that one can study and pass a test. The people going through these programs are not automatically getting ample experience. Consequently, a BCBA certificate no longer means that the holder has spent years working directly with various age groups within the autistic population, in a variety of settings.

When I have raised this issue within the professional autism community, I have certainly been met with the argument that BCBAs are well equipped to manage cases and design autism programs. In my consultation work, which involves in-depth reviews of clinical programs and clinical operations of service providers across the nation, I have observed too many service providers that only employ BCBAs to manage the clinical program and operations. Without a diverse professional group, including licensed clinical professionals with other areas of expertise and experience, it is highly unlikely that comprehensive behavior programs will be developed that meet the needs of their participants and comprehensively teach functional skills as well as all of the social and family aspects of developing relationships within the context of communities and our society. These programs lack an ecobehavioral approach, and their outcomes show it. In a well-intentioned effort to define best practices, the current ABA service provider market has become too rule-based, too short-sighted, and too self-serving. Individuals commonly express that ABA made them feel like a product more than a person. The intervention aims to extinguish and correct behaviors without necessarily understanding the source of those behaviors. For example, self-sensory stimulation, or "stimming," serves as an important release of anxiety and is a coping mechanism for many individuals with autism. As Christine explains, "Try not to tell them, 'Don't hand flap,' or 'Don't jump.' Because that's really how they calm their sensory system. Their sensory issues are basically ignored in the ABA world, especially anxiety."

These behaviors are often seen as abnormal, and service providers frequently devote a lot of energy to eliminating them, rather than understanding them. In this regard, we see an industry too fixated on the concept of normalizing autistic individuals—correcting their behavior to make them appear as if they are not autistic or removing odd behaviors that make them stand out. Eliminating the behavior without addressing the underlying function or anxiety causing the behavior is not effective long-term.

In a well-intentioned effort to define best practices, the current ABA service provider market has become too rule-based, too short-sighted, and too self-serving. Individuals commonly express that ABA made them feel like a product more than a person.

As many adults have described to me, one of their most difficult challenges in adulthood is managing the anxiety that comes with being autistic. The self-stimulatory behavior I am referring to here is not be confused with self-injurious behavior. I am not suggesting that we do not address self-injury, which can cause serious and long-term damage. Sometimes self-injury is an expression of pain or a medical issue, and medical issues should always be ruled out as an underlying cause. Understanding the function of a behavior, including whether it is sensory in nature, is the first step in understanding what is occurring for the individual and what should come next in intervention.

Another consequence of a rule-based, procedural approach is that it fails to teach dynamic thinking and problem-solving skills. Most skills are taught as a series of steps or processes that are based on rules. Children with autism are static thinkers—they think in a linear fashion and like the structure and stability of routine and predictability. Functionality in the world, however, demands being able to think and learn dynamically. That means learning should be adaptive and reflexive to interactions and environments. One has to adjust to routines that are constantly changing. One has to be able to walk into a situation and assess what is going on and how to react to it. Often, social skills programs are very time-limited and are not taught in a social environment; they are taught in a vacuum or with parents and siblings only. This is not nearly enough to equip individuals to be socially successful in the world and acquire the necessary skills to navigate employment and independence well.

While so much energy is devoted toward correcting the behaviors of those with autism, not enough resources are directed toward teaching the community how to understand and accept individuals with autism. Many autistic children experience bullying and feel ostracized as a result. A young man I met, Jared, put it brilliantly: "They said I had poor social skills, but what about the kids who were bullying me; don't they have poor social skills?" When bullying by the general community, by adults in workplaces, and by peers at school is seen as normal, and people instead focus on the behavior of those with autism, we can conclude that more efforts need to be centered on educating the rest of the student population and the community as a whole. Not all individuals affected by autism have intellectual disabilities; many are remarkably bright. But stigma and misunderstanding present barriers to them within the community. Jared expressed frustration over this, telling me, "I have to work ten times harder than you to be taken seriously." These social barriers limit autistic individuals' ability to provide meaningful contributions to the community, prevent them from obtaining jobs, and hinder their ability to form peer relationships.

THE IMPACT OF FUNDING

In order to effectively address these issues and better serve these individuals, we must understand how funding is affecting the industry and how to help facilitate a better funding model. As we discussed earlier in the book, autism services are part of a unique market where the payers are typically not those receiving the services. They receive funding for services via federal funding, state funding, or private insurance. However, under private insurance, families are responsible for copays and deductibles.

The funding landscape for autism and other disabilities is complex and ever-changing. Over the past years, new federal mandates and state funding laws have increased access to services and given families more opportunities to fund and access services. For example, the ABLE Act, signed into law in 2014, enables families to create tax-exempt 529A savings accounts for disability-related expenses, making it easier for families to save for their family member with a disability. Previously, these families may have faced the loss of federal benefits for doing so. Other states have passed legislation to increase funding in various programs, such as residential or community-based programs. In 2017, some state and federal funding was in question with the proposed plans to cut Medicaid over the next ten years.[41] Looking at the increase in diagnoses, the movement of individuals into community settings, and the rapidly expanding marketplace, it is necessary for funding to expand to meet the growing demand.

Over the past seventeen years, starting with Indiana in 2001, forty-six states and Washington, D.C. have enacted laws requiring insurance companies to cover the treatment of autism. This is a very positive trend, as increases in insurance funding for autism services mean more widespread recognition of the prevalence of autism and the need for families to be able to access essential services. The increase in legislation and funding streams also attracts the investment community. Increased funding has greatly expanded the accessibility of ABA to a much broader population, including those on Medicaid and children with private insurance. The shift to insurance has also helped define training standards and improved consumer protection. However, new challenges have arisen with increased involvement of insurance companies.

Insurance regulations differ from state to state. For example, ARICA, the insurance coverage law for autism services in Massachusetts, does not have any age, service, or dollar caps or limitations, whereas Colorado's law includes options to limit coverage based on age. Despite the legislative mandates that require insurance companies to provide autism services, actually receiving those services has not always been as easy as it would appear. ABA is relatively new to the insurance market in many states, and thus many insurance companies are unfamiliar with what ABA is, how best to fund it, or how to assess the quality of programs and adequately gauge outcomes.

---

41 Dylan Matthews, "Congress quietly passed a budget outline with $1.8 trillion in health care cuts," Vox, last modified October 26, 2017, https://www.vox.com/policy-and-politics/2017/10/26/16526458/2018-senate-budget-explained.

	Brief Description of Funding	What it Means
FEDERAL	The Individuals with Disabilities Education Act (IDEA) is a federal law, and the primary federal program, that provides educational and related services to children and adolescents with disabilities throughout the nation. Individuals between three and twenty-two years old who meet eligibility criteria qualify for necessary services to ensure a free and appropriate public education.	This may include ABA, speech therapy, occupational therapy, and other services as well as an Individualized Education Plan (IEP), which is a specific educational curriculum tailored to the individual needs and goals of each child.
MEDICAID	Medicaid is funded through the federal goverment, but each state has its own Medicaid program. Thus, Medicaid benefits are covered by both state and federal regulations. The federal Centers for Medicaid and Medicare Services (CMS) requires that states cover all medically necessary care for children with autism through age twenty-one. The obligation is part of the Early and Periodic Screening, Diagnostic, and Treatment benefit (EPSDT). EPSDT is a mandatory benefit and provides a comprehensive array of preventive, diagnositic, and treatment services for low-income infants, children, and adolescents under age twenty-one. CMS does not require any specific treatment for ASD. State agencies are responsible for determining medical necessity and treatments of choice.	Families have to be eligible for Medicaid coverage based on specific criteria. Examples of these criteria are: income level; participation in Supplemental Security Income (SSI); or because they are eligible through the Alternate Benefit Program (ABP). All children must receive EPSDT screenings designed to identify health and developmental issues, including ASD, as early as possible. This includes ruling out medical issues. Definitions for "medical necessity" may vary by state. Many states contract with private insurance companies or managed care organizations to manage their programs.
STATE	States have their own individual laws and regulations that provide for early intervention and services for individuals with developmental disabilities, mental health and physical disabilities. Some states provide a lifelong benefit while others provide services through adolescence and early adulthood. States contract with vendors, providers and community agencies to provide the necessary services.	Most states use a combination of diagnosis and functional assessment, and for adult services, financial qualification, to determine eligiblity for services. Many states provide specialized employment, job training, and placement for adults.
TRICARE	Insurance program that covers benefits and services for military families. TRICARE covers autism services through the TRICARE Comprehensive Autism Care Demonstration.	TRICARE funds Applied Behavior Analysis (ABA) intervention for all TRICARE beneficiaries diagnosed with autism spectrum disorder (ASD).
PRIVATE INSURANCE	Almost all states in the U.S. (currently forty-six and D.C.) have passed legislation requiring commercial insurance companies to cover certain kinds of autism-related interventions. With a diagnosis of ASD, the individual receives a functional behavior assessment to determine the need for services.	The requirements differ by state. Some laws have age caps or annual cost caps on autism intervention. Each company determines who they contract with, what types of services and programs they fund, and the intensity of program hours etc. The Mental Health Parity Act also requires that health plans treat mental health care, including autism-related care. Some insurance plans classify autism-related services as part of their "mental health" benefit.
PRIVATE PAY	Parents, family members, or others paying privately for services.	This generally comprises a very small percentage of funding for services.

The model of an intensive early intervention program—which requires from three to five or more hours of services per day, five days a week, for at least two years—is initially foreign to insurance companies. It does not fit the typical medical model of treatment. Learning and understanding the model of ABA services and rationale for intervention takes time and education, and while the shift to insurance has helped the medical community develop a better understanding of the treatment options for autism, this change in perspective is often slow.

Despite the decades of empirical evidence to support the efficacy of ABA interventions in autism, some insurance companies have classified ABA as "experimental" or "educational" in an attempt to deny coverage. In addition, some insurance companies are requiring testing that is not relevant to our industry or our intervention and is not sensitive enough to detect actual progress. Some of the testing is completely detached from what ABA does, such as some companies' focus on IQ testing as the major assessment for progress. This allows insurance companies to deny renewals of funding due to "lack of progress" or deny funding altogether due to "a child's IQ being too low for the child to benefit" from intervention.

An unfortunate result of this has been more and more service providers focusing on what they are being reimbursed for rather than what the science of ABA would mandate in a data-driven program. This lack of cohesion, combined with some insurance companies' unfamiliarity with ABA, is elevating inferior practices. The industry has to be more proactive in this regard. For example, one source told me that her service provider has stopped having monthly team meetings (where the entire team working with her child met to collaborate on her son's progress and program goals) because they are not being paid for them. This is an unfortunate development, as these kinds of meetings are an important component of coordination of care, program development, and progress.

Sadly, the larger players in the industry have not come to the table with health plans to shape the narrative on how care should be viewed and approached. The approach tends to be more of a self-serving one for the betterment of each individual company, and not for the service provider market and mission of the intervention as a whole.

I spoke with an industry insider named Brad, an expert on insurance funding, who further highlighted how a lack of industry standards is detrimental to the industry as a whole:

> *"The majority of ABA providers I have encountered are spending time, money, and energy working to ensure that their organizations are committed to providing the most comprehensive, ethical, and effective care for their clients. However, the handful of providers that are operating outside the clinical norm, cutting corners, committing fraud (intentionally or unintentionally)—[they] are causing the lion's share of the issues that will drive health plans to implement stronger regulations and standards that may not actually be the most appropriate for the industry and may harm care overall."*

Any such regulations or standards that are imposed through health plans will not be beneficial to providers or those receiving services, simply because those writing the regulations are not basing them on ABA standards of care or practice.

While increased access is something that should be applauded, little to no funding exists for indirect services such as indirect supervision (supervision provided to a direct care provider outside of an intervention session), program development and modification, and often report-writing, which are critical components of successful interventions based on best practice standards of care. This largely falls on the provider market—we have done a poor job advocating for the correct funding to support quality programs. By accepting low rates forced on the industry by payers, providers are actually hurting the industry.

As discussed, standardization of clinical outcome measures and procedures presents a whole other issue. The industry standard has become "providers protect their methods and their outcomes as a means of gaining an advantage on their competition." Put another way, proprietary interests are obstructing the necessary process of establishing clear, standardized approaches and measures of outcomes. Because each company is so focused on protecting its methods, there is no consistency in how outcomes are measured, and thus no standards in how insurance companies assess programs.

Brad expressed fear that the lack of consensus between providers and the lack of clearly defined industry outcomes could significantly hurt the industry moving forward:

> *"I think the health plans see this as a glaring need to the management puzzle. As discussed before, the providers as a whole lack a true consensus on how treatment should be approached as it relates to recommended hours, caregiver involvement, reducing service hours and fading out intervention, exit from ABA treatment, and alternate appropriate types of care. This lack of cohesion limits the industry's ability to collect and produce true outcome data. In my opinion, this may present itself as a real barrier to providers moving forward, as they*

will lose their ability to control care as MCOs [managed care organizations] will look to dictate standards of care."

The industry must find ways to address critical deficits in training models by establishing common standards around outcome measures. Failing to do so will essentially turn control of our industry over to third parties that have little to no understanding of the science or our goals. I know several individuals in the professional community who are working hard to achieve this goal, trying to collaborate with providers to measure outcomes consistently and share data. All have shared their frustration at how unwilling the majority of service provider companies are when it comes to sharing and comparing to achieve this important goal.

Increased funding from insurance companies has been a very important development for the industry and for individuals who need autism services. Many good people have fought long and hard to break down walls and enable these funding channels. However, there is much work to be done to elevate best practices and improve the funding models to ensure that the right program components are being funded and outcomes are being properly assessed.

When examining outcomes of autism services, the focus must also be on the long-term outcomes for individuals. To assess long-term outcomes, I examined areas integral to independent living and happiness. These areas include living situation, community participation, health, and personal relationships. When we take a critical look at these outcomes, what is revealed is troubling.

FAQ:
___

WHAT ARE SOME BARRIERS TO ENTRY WHEN LOOKING TO INVEST?

Many investors require a target of substantial size. The current autism provider landscape is highly fragmented and consists mainly of thousands of very small businesses, many growing faster than they can manage.

Finding the right initial investment platform:

While there is a strong logic to consolidate the market, finding the right initial company upon which to build the platform is key. This includes the quality of clinical methodology and approach to services, the management, the reputation, regulatory compliance, and the financial performance of the company.

Public payer concentration:

Even within larger companies, there is public payer concentration which present risks due to rate cuts and potential legislative changes.

Lack of diversity in market and geography:

Many providers have market concentration and lack proof of concept and repeatability of success in other markets.

Inability or lack of proof of ability to recruit staff to support growth initiatives:

Currently, there is a shortage of BCBAs (board-certified behavior analysts) in many regions. BCBAs are required to provide supervision in most markets. This constraint inhibits growth.

Strength of infrastructure:

Even within the larger companies, many lack the systems, management, and infrastructure to support scaling a platform. Most ABA services companies have yet to transition to a professionally managed healthcare model.

WHAT'S MISSING FROM OUTCOMES?

We've touched on outcomes in several places, because they are so critical, but we haven't really taken a critical examination of what we know as an industry. In the rest of this chapter, I will provide an overview of challenges the industry faces concerning outcomes and take a critical look at long-term outcomes in the areas of employment, social activity, health, living situations, and personal relationships.

There are several issues concerning outcomes in the services field that need to be addressed: understanding how outcomes factor into insurance models, taking a critical look at long-term outcomes, and acknowledging that current models are failing many individuals.

Most pressing, the industry needs to understand that outcomes are essential to insurance funding. As Brad explained, "Insurance companies, like most funding agencies, are interested in providing services that produce good outcomes and reduce costs for further care."

If the industry is not able to come together and define those outcomes, they will be defined for us by insurance management teams who do not fully appreciate the essential components of services. It cannot be stressed enough how critical it is for providers across the industry to come together, communicate with each other, and establish agreed-upon practices for measuring and evaluating outcomes. Competitive inclinations need to be set aside, and standards must be determined. Failure to do so prevents us from clearly assessing how well we are doing and effectively finding ways to improve, as well as differentiating providers.

Currently, companies do not generally focus on long-term outcomes and instead focus mainly on short-term outcomes. Clinicians assess how many objects a child can identify before and after an intervention session, or how quickly a child meets a specific goal, but they don't assess the child's ability to function in the world using those skills. How many obtain the skills needed to live on their own, or are able to hold jobs? How many have meaningful personal relationships? This is an area in which we can all empathize. Human relationships are important to all of us and can be challenging to maintain. For individuals with autism, that challenge is much more daunting. As Christine said of autism and life, "You know, autism is hard ... but so is being human." That quote beautifully captures her resilience and hits at the commonalities we all share.

These are critical areas of living a full life, yet providers largely ignore them. Sometimes, this is inadvertently caused by parental pressure and parents being reluctant or too stressed by current daily challenges to have the long-term conversation. No matter the reason, this is a myopic view that fails to account for what these children will need as adults.

In this regard, many providers are neglecting what the true aim of services should be. In my work examining service providers, I have seen providers set minimal goals, goals which are not socially valid,[42] and goals that are not relevant. Many families are not knowledgeable consumers when it comes to assessing providers and their programs, leaving them vulnerable to receiving poor service.

Another area that seems to be overlooked is caregiver (parents, grandparents, babysitters etc.) outcomes. Caregivers already face numerous challenges. It is more than difficult to navigate the needs of their children, work, and other responsibilities. I understand this reality and do not wish to downplay their situations. However, getting involved in their child's program and learning the techniques

---

42 *Social validity* refers to the social importance, appropriateness, and acceptability of intervention goals, procedures, and outcomes.

will ultimately result in better outcomes and prognoses. Data on caregivers is critical; they should have their own goals in terms of learning and applying intervention techniques. Their goals should be functional, objective, measurable, and specific. For intervention to be successful, caregivers must be able to apply methods in an ongoing, consistent manner.

Interestingly, upon examination of a large sample of parent feedback on the services they were receiving, parents who were not involved gave extremely high satisfaction scores when rating their service provider. Parents who were involved in intervention and required to participate at some level gave satisfaction scores that were still high, but slightly lower than the non-participating groups. When discussing this data with the researchers, it is evident that very high family satisfaction scores across a provider generally indicated that parents or other caregivers were not required to be present for intervention. Having parents present is absolutely vital. Research demonstrates that parental involvement in intervention improves outcomes for children. These researchers also indicated the gross failure across many providers to properly collect data enabling a true assessment of outcomes.

I believe that when companies shift their focus from only short-term outcomes to both short-term and long-term outcomes, the picture will become much more urgent. Drexel University conducted a comprehensive study of individuals with developmental disabilities in 2017. Their National Autism Indicators Report details some alarming numbers about how well adults with autism are faring in the community. It is imperative that the industry take a close look at these statistics and ask what we can do to improve them.

Let's dig into long-term outcomes, focusing on key areas of functionality, civic participation, and happiness. To assess long-term outcomes, I have focused on employment and social activity, health, living situations and independence, and peer relationships.

EMPLOYMENT AND SOCIAL ACTIVITY

The Drexel University study revealed that only 14 percent of autistic adults surveyed had paid, community-based employment, with 54 percent participating in unpaid activities in a facility (day habilitation centers for adults with disabilities, supervised work programs for individuals with developmental disabilities, etc.).[43] Most individuals are either in day programs or at home. This has multiple effects, including profound effects on self-esteem and emotional issues, as lack of employment hinders these individuals' ability to meaningfully participate in their communities.

The study showed that over 30 percent of autistic adults ages eighteen to twenty-nine, and over 17 percent of autistic adults ages thirty to sixty-four, have community-based employment goals in their service plans but cannot find or maintain jobs. Either they don't have the skills they need to do so, or stigma deters potential employers. Likely, it is a combination of social stigmatization, bullying, and the poor treatment individuals with disabilities face that precludes these individuals from the job market.

A job provides individuals with meaningful social activity, the opportunity to contribute to society, and the opportunity to be compensated for their skills and abilities—things that are lacking for many autistic individuals. It also helps individuals form a positive self-image and contributes to self-worth. In lieu of a job, meaningful

---

43 Anne M. Roux, Jessica E. Rast, Kristy A. Anderson, and Paul T. Shattuck. *National Autism Indicators Report: Developmental Disability Services and Outcomes in Adulthood*. Philadelphia, PA: Life Course Outcomes Program, A.J. Drexel Autism Institute, Drexel University, 2017.

social activity could help. However, out of those surveyed, 27 percent had no work or even day activities in the two weeks prior to the survey. That kind of inactivity is not mentally or emotionally healthy. It's no wonder that 41 percent of respondents reported feeling lonely.

Many individuals would benefit from support groups, but due to the stigma associated with the disorder, not many exist, and self-advocacy organizations are often slow to respond to requests. One self-advocate discussed why such support networks don't exist in the autism community.

> *"Once you're an adult, you don't have to disclose the diagnosis, and that's why there's not too many support groups ... So, that contributes to isolation ... [I]t's like a double-edged sword. You don't want to tell people what's going on with you but then you can't get the support that you need."*

HEALTH

According to the Drexel study, over half (54 percent) of adults with autism suffer from at least one mental health condition, including anxiety, depression, or behavioral challenges. While these conditions may be innate, some may be caused or at least exacerbated by isolation and lack of physical activity. Of course, mental illness can make working, living independently, and participating in the community more difficult.

More than half (58 percent) also had body mass indices that placed them in the overweight or obese category, putting them at higher risk for a myriad of critical health conditions. Is the industry paying enough attention to teaching these individuals proper diet and exercise? Are they getting enough activity in their daily lives, or are they living sedentary lifestyles? A mom I spoke with observed that teaching individuals with disabilities about fitness and health seems altogether absent from most programs. These questions need to be examined, because failing to do so is failing to address issues that will drastically impact autistic adults' life expectancy and quality.

LIVING SITUATION AND INDEPENDENCE

One of the most troubling statistics in the report is that only 10 percent of adults with autism live in an independent home. Nearly half (49 percent) live in the home of a parent or relative. Nearly 40 percent of those living at home received no paid in-home support services, and of those who received no support, 37 percent indicated they needed some type of support services. Is living at home with a parent or relative throughout adulthood really a measure of long-term success? While this may seem preferable to institutionalization, it is not a tenable situation. What happens when their parents or relatives pass on? Would their lives not be markedly better if they were living independent lives in a community of their choice?

In addition to the respondents who lived independently or in a family home, 27 percent of those surveyed lived in group homes, 8 percent lived in institutions, and 5 percent were listed as having "other" living arrangements. When examined by age, young adults were more likely to live with family members. In the forty-five to sixty-four-year-old age group, 20 percent were living in institutions, and 40 percent were living in group homes.

Of the total group of adults surveyed, few chose their own home or who lived with them. Sixteen percent of adults chose where to live and 17 percent chose their roommate. Sixty percent reported that the choice of where to live was made for them. This question was not asked of individuals who lived at home.

Fewer than half (43 percent) of the adults who responded chose their own schedules regarding when they woke up, ate, or went to sleep. That means nearly six out of ten have so little autonomy that they are not even deciding these basic choices themselves. Choice is a very important facet of life and independence. We live in a choice-driven world, and the industry needs to focus more effort on equipping the individuals we work with to function in that world.

It's clear that the industry needs to do a better job preparing individuals for adult life, and services are going to have to be developed to help individuals currently living in untenable situations. As long as we ignore these long-term realities, they will remain a blind spot in services.

RELATIONSHIPS

Often, individuals living with autism experience considerable difficulty forming interpersonal relationships. While the Drexel study found that 72 percent of respondents reported having at least one friend who was not a family member or caregiver, the data provided no context as to the substance of those relationships or the frequency of contact.

Other studies[44] have found that around 46 percent of adolescents and adults with autism have no peer relationships. Of those who did have one or more peer relationships, the frequency of contact was

---

44 Mark Stokes, Naomi Newton, and Archana Kaur, *Stalking, and Social and Romantic Functioning Among Adolescents and Adults with Autism Spectrum Disorder,* Burwood, Australia: School of Psychology, Faculty of Health, Medicine, Nursing, and Behavioural Sciences, Deakin University, 2007.

inversely correlated to the degree of social impairment. These studies also show, despite previous misconceptions, that autistic individuals' desire for interpersonal and romantic relationships was similar to the general population.

Because autistic individuals have problems interpreting social cues, they may have trouble determining or communicating their own emotions, may exhibit unconventional social behaviors, and may have an aversion to touch, making forming relationships quite difficult. Further complicating the matter, many have an inability to separate appropriate and inappropriate social behavior. For example, while it is normal for two people who are attracted to one another to exchange glances and quick smiles, an autistic person may stare too long or smile too big. Behaviors such as calling or e-mailing someone are acceptable, but only in moderation. For autistic individuals, it is often difficult to sense where the line is between appropriate and off-putting, or even behaviors that mimic stalking.

. . . .

Social Skills Programs

Social skills are foundational skills related to communication, social interactions, problem-solving, decision-making, self-management, and peer interactions. These critical skills enable one to form and maintain positive relationships, manage classroom and community settings, and later in life, find and maintain a job, attend college, and form and maintain friendships and romantic relationships.

One's social competence is directly related to social acceptance, inclusion, independence, and success at many daily tasks.

Social skills programs teach skills such as making eye contact, greeting, the use of body language, effective communication, initiating conversations, cooperation, and flexibility.

. . . .

Christine articulated how, despite all her achievements, ABA has not been very effective at helping her socially interact with others. In college, when she would try to engage socially with her peers, she discovered that the ways she had been taught to interact with people weren't working.

> *"How do you implement [social skills]? When nobody else was taught these skills, these rules. The people you're having a conversation with—not everybody is going to follow the social rules that you were taught in social skills classes or ABA."*

Currently, few autism intervention programs emphasize and facilitate the practice of these important social dynamics. But this is an imperative part of human existence and is necessary for a happy life. If the industry wishes to help those living with autism to live full and meaningful lives, we must find ways to better enable them to form lasting peer relationships.

WHAT'S AT STAKE?

ABA has been a marvel of progress. It has broken through barriers and found ways to engage and teach autistic individuals. It helped Christine and others like her achieve the skills to succeed academically in college and in some important areas of adulthood. However, it failed to teach her valuable social skills and help her gain full independence. ABA is powerful, but it can also be limiting if it is not used optimally or not focused on appropriate long-term goals. There are many adults with autism who are disengaged from the world; the implementation of ABA has made significant progress for many individuals, but these accomplishments don't always translate into comprehensive adult successes.

Providers need to be nimble and cooperative—only by coming together and sharing data and techniques can we really standardize best practices and ensure that payers are funding what actually works. Providers need to take control of their industry, or insurance companies who do not fully appreciate the nuances of ABA and the science upon which it is based will dictate terms to them. For investors, understanding this will help them invest in companies that can take a proactive role in reshaping the industry so that funding is informed and effective.

It's important to understand that self-advocates, from teens to adults, have a powerful and growing voice. They are being vocal about what has worked for them and what has not. Investors and providers need to heed these calls, because these self-advocates demand something that better meets their needs. The demand in the market will shift, and providers need to be prepared to meet the new demand.

The industry also has to be bold enough to ask, what comes next? We have to be willing to have the conversation about how to use the technology and the methodology that ABA provides us to expand our teaching and develop ways to impart a comprehensive set of skills individuals need to function in the world. The industry can't focus only on short-term outcomes and ignore the real-world consequences these individuals face as adults. The industry has to be honest about where we are so we can improve and move forward. It needs to move outside of the current "walls" of ABA as we know them to include the skills people need to function in the world. Millions of individuals, the industry that serves them, and our communities depend on it.

CHAPTER 5

WHY IS IT TIME TO JUMP THE S-CURVE?

Most successful businesses follow a pattern of growth and decline known as an *S-curve*. They start small and improve once they find their market and the right business formula. Then performance accelerates rapidly, as consumers learn about the product or service and the offering is refined and matures. Eventually, they hit a peak, where the market is saturated and competitors or imitators appear. Improvement stalls, and often external factors compound to make their existing model stagnate or become obsolete. If the business does not evolve and innovate, stagnation and decline are likely. This happens in every industry, and businesses must evolve to survive. However, some industries have more difficulty evolving than others.

The delivery models of care in the healthcare industry are generally known for evolving slowly and utilizing outdated

TOPICS AHEAD:

WHAT IS AN S-CURVE?

WHAT HAPPENS TO EXECUTIVES?

COMPANIES AND INDUSTRIES THAT HAVE MADE THE JUMP

THE PURSUIT

systems that are inefficient, consume big budgets, and have individuals making decisions about funding who have limited to no experience delivering the care. That is not to say it is impossible.

Take Amedisys as an example. It was started in 1982 as a healthcare staffing company but soon began to offer other services. It ran surgery and post-acute care centers and grew fast, operating over three hundred facilities in eight states by 1995. All was going well until President Clinton signed the Balanced Budget Act. The law established a fixed-payment system that cut home health reimbursement retroactively by a staggering 50 percent. In the blink of an eye, external forces completely changed the industry in which Amedisys was thriving.

Desperate for answers and considering bankruptcy, Amedisys was forced to rethink its business model. To successfully jump the S-curve, it would focus on home healthcare, with special emphasis on disease management for an aging population. With new regulations threatening to put home health agencies out of business, Amedisys had to find a way to streamline services and deliver home healthcare quicker, cheaper, and more effectively than its competitors.

The transition wasn't easy. The company had to sell off its staffing division, surgery centers, and physician services business. That meant terminating employees and reallocating those resources. But it paid off for the company—over the next two years, one-third of all home care agencies shut their doors, while Amedisys went on to become one of the top-performing public companies in the nation. Amedisys successfully jumped to their second S-curve. Now, with the realities of the Affordable Care Act and an uncertain future for national healthcare legislation, Amedisys is keeping an eye to the future, aware that it may soon have to jump another S-curve.

There comes a time in every industry, for every company, when evolution is necessary. In the field of autism services, that time is here. The ABA service model is good; it has served many thousands of young people and has transformed lives. However, if we do not honestly assess its deficits and how to progress and evolve, we will—sooner rather than later—fall to outside forces. Such is the nature of all business. In this chapter, we frame the current issues in ABA services by detailing how they represent external influences that will force the industry of autism services to evolve.

The time has come for the autism services industry to build a new vision and build off of what has been accomplished. While investors are very familiar with S-curves and business cycles, autism service providers are often, first and foremost, clinicians. This chapter is aimed at helping providers understand how industries cycle and how investors look at businesses in terms of life cycles.

WHAT IS AN S-CURVE?

Put simply, the S-curve traces the investment, growth, and downslope of development and industry, on a graph of performance over time. The concept of jumping the S-curve is the secret to high-performing and long-lasting businesses. By the time their existing business model starts to stall (the downslope of the S-curve), they are already busy developing their new model. This allows them to beat downward trends that naturally occur for any product, business, or industry.

Take a look at the graphic on the next page, and you'll see three distinct regions of the S-curve. You have your initial bucket, or drop, where resources are being expended to create and develop a business. That is followed by an uptrend, where the initial investment pays off. The uptrend is when business is growing and you are able to scale.

But inevitably, that upward trend breaks, momentum is lost, and the curve slopes downward.

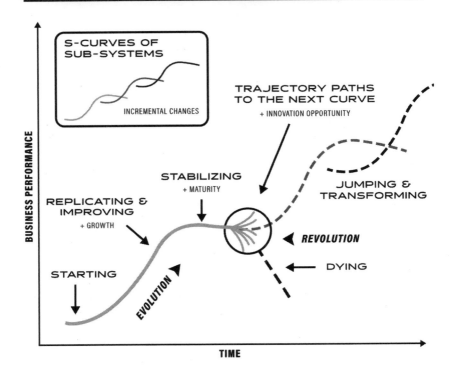

HIGH PERFORMERS JUMP S-CURVES

The key to long-term survival is finding a new model and developing it before your current model loses its momentum. The highest-performing companies and industries are S-curve jumpers. They possess the critical mind-set to see that downward slope coming and get ahead of it. I have been in executive and management meetings where the team is asked to identify where the company is on the S-curve, and it is interesting how different managers and executives, with different lenses into the business, will place the company at different stages. I believe that we are close to the top of the curve in ABA services. While there is much growth to be had in the industry, if providers want to remain relevant and respond to shifting market demands, it is time to start developing our next model—the next evolution of autism services.

First, we will look at the leaders responsible for jumping the S-curve and discuss common reasons why many leaders, businesses, and industries fail to make that jump. Then we will look outside autism services to other industries that have successfully jumped the S-curve in the past to demonstrate that the concept is a reality many business must contend with, regardless of the industry. Finally, we will consider our shared goals and lay out what needs to be done if we are going to successfully make the jump.

WHAT HAPPENS TO EXECUTIVES?

While evolving and jumping the S-curve seems like the sensible thing to do, there is a lot of pressure on business leaders and executives to not evolve or pivot. As a leader, you are focused on managing the strategy and execution of all the practices that govern the cycle of service or product delivery, the multitude of administrative tasks (such as talent acquisition, training, and retention), and the design of operational systems to support growth. Executives are

If a CEO gets stuck in the daily details, it's easy to lose sight of the bigger pictures and what's happening in the marketplace.

concerned with the key indicators of company profit, growth, revenue cycle management, and achieving a competitive edge. While a CEO's primary role is to focus on these big-picture tasks and overall metrics, many CEOs and executives—myself included—have struggled with the daily fires that need putting out and the details that can take away our attention. A business's day-to-day demands can get in the way.

From my experience as a CEO, I've learned the struggle is best described as "working *in* the company" versus "working *on* the company." As a CEO, our job is to get our nose out of the day-to-day, look into the future and work on the company. If a CEO gets stuck in the daily details, it's easy to lose sight of the bigger picture and what's happening in the marketplace. This can lead companies to fail to jump the S-curve.

I experienced this need to remind myself to work on my company throughout my time with AST. In the early days of the business, we were developing a model that worked and that differentiated us in the marketplace—a way to make a meaningful difference in the lives of individuals with autism and their families and to help them reach their fullest potential. Years of education and experience formed what would become the model for the ABA services we provided at AST. It worked. The schools and state agencies saw that it worked, the parents saw that it worked, and we experienced great success. We were able to scale and become one of the largest service providers in California at that time and I was deeply involved in the day-to-day decisions and processes of service delivery.

When the financial crisis hit the markets in 2008, the climate changed in California. Payers started decreasing the number of hours they would fund for programs and newly diagnosed families were placed on long waiting lists to be assessed for services. We sensed that payers were going to start focusing intensely on service delivery models, reimbursement, and additional potential cost-saving measures. With this anticipated change in the market, we began working on strategies to reorganize the company and innovate our clinical model to lower costs. When the state of California passed down retroactive cuts to funding, we had to instantly change our clinical operations. There was a high level of uncertainty. By pulling away from the day-to-day and focusing strategically on where the business needed to be to survive, I saw we needed to rapidly pivot and innovate to maintain cash flow, meet payroll, remain profitable, and retain our position in the market. Preserving the quality of our clinical model while working to retain staff and simultaneously revamping our clinical operations to cut costs was an extremely stressful and challenging period. Questions about how to preserve the integrity of our model piled up on top of staffing, turnover, profit, and loss. I didn't have all the answers, and that terrified me. What ultimately helped was seeing my role as CEO not in the day-to-day—or as someone who has all the answers—but rather the big picture: someone who didn't have the answers but knew to ask the team, and other individuals who could offer support, where to find them.

When you're in an executive position, people depend on you to either have answers or know which questions to ask. Their very livelihoods depend on your ability to successfully run the company and provide employees with gainful employment. Like everyone else, CEOs work with the information that they have and often doubt their decision-making and leadership abilities. Many CEOs are comfortable admitting their vulnerabilities while sitting around a table with other executives, but few are ready to share those vulnerabilities with their employees. Because human beings are psychologically hard-wired to avoid embarrassment, not having the answers and showing vulnerability when you're in a position of authority can be very stressful. Some will pretend to have the answers, while others will just focus on what they know to be true and may spin things to shift the focus. I was encouraged to be honest, showcase my vulnerability, and admit to not having all the answers.

After an extremely difficult period of change as we adapted to this new world of funding and rate cuts, I gathered the courage to tell our employees exactly what we had faced. They were questioning some of the changes we made within the company, such as layoffs and organizational restructuring, often pointing fingers at management for "changing our minds and reverting decisions" or "not appreciating employees." I explained the rationale for some of our decisions and the fact that we were pivoting, as the funding sources were making unexpected changes that had significant ripple effects to clinical operations. We often were not given a runway on which to do this elegantly. The goal was to preserve the entire company and ensure our long-term sustainability. I exposed the fact that I did not have all the answers and was trying to figure it out with the information I had. I laid bare my concerns and told them what we could guarantee and what we couldn't. It was an incredibly difficult thing to do, to be so vulnerable and open with them, with the fear that transparency would result in resignations and doubt.

But something remarkable happened after that exchange. People felt unburdened, as if it were okay for them to be honest and open as well about where they were struggling within their departments. Authenticity breeds authenticity. Once I opened up to people, they felt more connected to me and the company. That's the moment when everything changed, the conversation became open, and our people became fully invested and aligned with our mission. Our culture changed, our ability to adapt and grow as a team improved, and we successfully jumped our S-curve.

It wasn't our first time doing so. We jumped our first S-curve at AST when we took PRT and other naturalistic intervention strategies and applied them to an intensive in-home therapy model. Prior to doing so, we were providing school-based services mostly focused on improving behavior and social skills. We were approached by the state of California to develop an innovative model to meet the needs of intensive, in-home service delivery on a large scale that was family-focused and required parent and caregiver participation with fewer service delivery hours but equal or better outcomes. The clinical methodology was not new for us, but the approach we took to delivering in-home services was much different than what was mainstream at the time. We jumped the S-curve and brought a successful retail model of naturalistic intervention into the mainstream market.

We faced considerable backlash for daring to question the conventional belief that therapy must be provided in a rigid, forty-plus-hour-per-week structure. A vocal opposition was telling parents that if they used services from AST, they would be damaging their children. However, we addressed the market in a different way, innovating and developing a program that produced as-effective results in fewer hours. That was the key to our success, and if we had hesitated to jump that S-curve, it never would have happened.

Yet, when it came time to do it again years later, when we were established and a much larger company, I hesitated to be open and vulnerable with our people. I had to overcome the fear that was holding me back and be genuine with my team to find a way forward. What I had failed to appreciate in the early days of running AST was the importance of company culture and its impact on business success. I learned over time that your company will develop a culture by default if you do not intentionally create a culture by design. When we started AST, we had a very specific mission to provide high-quality, family-focused, individualized programs that made truly meaningful changes in the lives of our clients and their families. Our mission never changed. But our culture got in the way of achieving our strategic goals. When we put ourselves through the systematic exercises of truly defining our culture and how we were going to conduct ourselves, starting with myself as CEO, our company transformed.

The conversations we were able to have once we transformed our culture were inspiring and heartening. Success came with continued growth, and when we faced the next S-curve jump—adapting our model once again to accommodate the shifting funding landscape, when commercial insurance entered our market—we were much better poised to recognize the need for innovation and to do what needed to be done. Ultimately, when the time was right for us, we made the decision to sell the company.

The link between strategy and culture is inextricable: if you don't have a strong culture, you cannot execute on your strategy. What is apparent in the current autism investment landscape is the frequent lack of attention to company culture by investors post-acquisition, which often sabotages success and results in the loss of clinical professionals.

FAQ:

WHAT SHOULD PROVIDERS CONSIDER WHEN SELLING ALL OR PART OF THEIR BUSINESS?

Bringing on an investor to buy a portion, or all, of one's company is one of the biggest decisions an entrepreneur will make in his or her life. Here are some of the major considerations when doing so:

- The first decision, and one of the most important ones, is how much of the company to sell. Depending on whether you sell a minority stake, majority stake, or 100 percent of your company will dictate the type of investor, the structure of the deal, and the level to which you will need to be involved with, committed to, and aligned with the buyer.

- Private equity buyers are generally more inclined to work with the seller than strategic buyers who typically want the seller uninvolved with the business post-close. However, replacement of executive team members is common post-close.

- It is highly recommended to engage an experienced broker or investment banker and legal counsel who are experienced and equipped to promote seller's interests during the deal process. The goal for the seller is to preserve deal value as the sale process ensues.

- Examining the potential investor's track record and speaking with owners of previous companies purchased by the investor is essential.

- The cultural fit between the seller's company and buyer is critical to the long-term success of the merger. Most investors will say that culture matters, but few invest the time and resources to assess the culture and truly understand it. Likewise, many founders don't truly see their company culture as it is, and many overestimate how the company culture transcends the founder. When cultures are not aligned, retention often suffers which impacts growth and profitability.

- Understanding how much and where the investor intends to invest resources is significant. Often, the programs that founders care about will be discarded by investors. Similarly, investors may not be planning to invest the needed capital into processes, clinical models, and growth that is required to scale the business long-term and achieve the goals set by the buyer.

One reason I was compelled to write this book is because I believe the time has come for the industry to evolve and make that jump to the next S-curve. I want to empower investors and providers so they can, in turn, empower the autistic community. When we recognize the need to evolve and make a conscious effort to do so, significant downturns can be avoided by making the jump when we must. All of the longest-lasting companies and industries have done this. The value and understanding of working on the business versus in the business was vital to the sustainability and growth of our company by ensuring that transformation, change, and complex problem solving was occurring. For context, let's analyze a few examples that demonstrate this trend and how making the jump to the next S-curve is a fundamental for all businesses.

COMPANIES AND INDUSTRIES THAT HAVE MADE THE JUMP

While investors understand S-curves and know how commonly companies are forced to jump them, I want to demonstrate this to providers using some high-profile examples of companies making those jumps.

In 1981, Bill Gates and a team of engineers released MS-DOS, the Microsoft Disc Operating System. Before they could take it to market, they invested time and money in it—the initial bucket on the S-curve. Then it took off. IBM took it and built it into their computers, and Microsoft saw phenomenal revenue growth. MS-DOS made using computers easier and played a key role in spurring the personal computer revolution. Then something happened.

A small company named Apple released a commercially available computer with something called a graphical user interface (GUI).

GUIs had been around, but Apple completely changed the personal computing market when they released a machine featuring one. This was an external force—something completely out of Microsoft's control. Suddenly, not because Microsoft was doing anything wrong but because the landscape had simply changed, MS-DOS was no longer the future.

DOS would continue to be manufactured until 2000, but by the time Microsoft ceased making it, they had already well established its replacement. Microsoft Windows is now the definitive model for PC operating systems. Did Microsoft wait until MS-DOS was

The industry must jump to its new S-curve and prepare to meet the shifting demand for a new type of service and improved outcomes that translate to quality of life.

not as popular to develop Windows? No, they started developing Windows just a few years after MS-DOS was rolled out because Apple's GUI forced them to.

Initially, Windows was just an extension of MS-DOS, but soon it would become the main operating system of personal computers. Microsoft again had to invest and make it through the initial dip in the S-curve. It wasn't until Windows 3.0, released in 1990, that Windows really started to take off. But then it really took off, and Microsoft was able to catch a huge vertical.

The innovation of Windows wasn't because MS-DOS was bad. In fact, MS-DOS was remarkable—it was a user-based computer operating system that achieved massive success. But just because a product is good doesn't mean it doesn't have to evolve. That's important to keep in mind as we look at the current ABA model of autism services.

Then external factors once again changed the game for Microsoft. With the advent of the Internet, people suddenly weren't as concerned with operating systems. Microsoft again successfully jumped the S-curve with Internet Explorer.

Now on Windows 10 and Internet Explorer 11, Microsoft has shown its ability to jump the S-curve, and that's why it remains a dominant force in its industry.

Apple is one of the best innovators and S-curve jumpers of our time. They took the world by surprise with the iPod, the iPhone, and the Apple watch which have revolutionized how we operate. Apple is a computer company that has become a lifestyle company. They have clearly defined the "why" of what they do, and their culture is a key factor in their success. Their values of excellence, innovation, and secrecy have supported them in becoming the market leader.

S-curve jumpers can be observed in any industry. Companies like Amazon, Black & Decker, and Procter & Gamble are great examples. They're always ahead of the curve when it comes to transitioning to a new model. That's why they remain relevant and dominate as the world continues to change and markets evolve.

More relevant to the ABA field, entire industries follow this trend of having to jump the curve and evolve. Consider a new luxury car and compare it to the original Model T. The Model T was an engineering feat which revolutionized transportation. But the industry as a whole has continued to evolve. Today's cars are safer, faster, more comfortable, and more efficient. There have been countless jumps from the Model T to the automobiles of today, and the industry will continue to make jumps as the world changes. Environmental concerns have birthed hybrid and electric cars. Now, driverless cars are starting to appear on the road, and flying cars are in development and have very recently been showcased.

Alternatively, let's look at companies that ignored where they were on the S-curve and failed. When Netflix first formed, its founder proposed a partnership to Blockbuster that was completely dismissed by Blockbuster's CEO. Ten years later, Blockbuster filed for bankruptcy and Netflix disrupted the video market. Blockbuster's CEO failed to see how Netflix's model would disrupt the market and Blockbuster's revenue model. A similar story occurred with Toys "R" Us and Amazon. These examples are more relevant because these companies, while providing specific products, are also service companies. Netflix disrupted the service delivery model of movie rentals, as did Amazon with toys and other products. These examples across industries demonstrate that companies that fail to make the jump to the next S-curve risk failure.

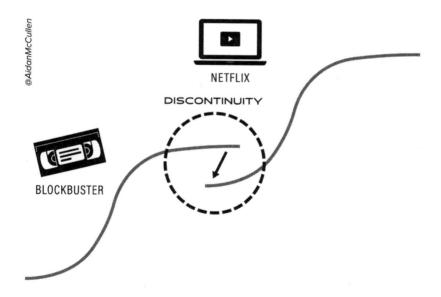

In the autism services industry, we are facing our own external factors that will force us to jump the curve or face decline: a maturing population of individuals with autism who do not possess the skills needed to care for themselves, and an aging population of parents and relatives who care for them and will eventually pass on. Furthermore, hundreds of thousands of teens with autism will become adults in the next decade, many of whom will not have the skills they need to live independent lives. And payers, especially commercial insurance, are beginning to dictate how we should conduct our services and what we should measure. In light of these realities, combined with self-advocates and caregivers increasingly critiquing many of the current ABA models of service delivery, the industry must jump to its new S-curve and prepare to meet the shifting demand for a new type of service and improved outcomes that translate to quality of life.

THE PURSUIT

As an industry, we must ask ourselves: What are we pursuing? Is it financial gains? Is it scalability? Or is it the best way to help autistic individuals and transform lives? Yes, success is important for sustainability and financial growth, but it's important because it enables us to reach more people and provide better services to those who need them.

Now ask the question: Is failing to share data with one another aiding in that pursuit? Does a lack of standards and clearly defined, measurable outcomes aid in that pursuit? Is the inability of service providers to define their own metrics, leading outside forces to do so for them, a good business strategy? I think much of the industry has developed a myopic view and is operating in a growth mind-set. The industry has to shake off the blinders and see the larger issues our market is facing. It must come together on these critical issues so it can effectively make the jump to the next S-curve.

In this sense, autism services are unique. Competition drove other industries to make their jumps and evolve. But because autism services are dependent on a third-party payer system, lack of cohesion presents an obstacle that will prevent us from finding our next S-curve. If we don't collaborate and communicate more effectively, share information, and establish standard outcome measures, for example, insurance companies will do it for us and, as we detailed in the last chapter, they mostly do not possess the knowledge or understanding to do so effectively. The results will prove detrimental to the industry and our ability to serve autistic individuals.

The time has come for autism services to evolve. Once we define objective outcomes, different approaches and models will help us determine best practices and build off of them. Then we will be free to determine what should come next. How do we take the individuals we serve beyond where the current model of ABA intervention is bringing them?

ABA has served us well, just as DOS served Microsoft and the personal computing industry well. Acknowledging that we are now in a position to do better does not detract from the amazing feats the ABA service community has accomplished. It's time to innovate and find the next S-curve before the current uptrend takes its inevitable downturn.

CHAPTER 6

EMPOWERING INVESTORS, PROVIDERS, AND COMMUNITIES

Donald Triplett was born in Forest, Mississippi, in 1933.[45] At an early age, it was evident that Donald demonstrated keen abilities for counting, memorization, music, and measuring. He also had some characteristics and behaviors that caused concern

---

45 Richard Pallardy, "Donald Triplett,"
Encyclopaedia Britannica,
https://www.britannica.com/biography/
Donald-Triplett.

TOPICS AHEAD:

INVESTORS: SOCIAL IMPACT
THROUGH FINANCIAL INVESTMENT

SERVICE PROVIDERS: MEETING
THE SHIFTING DEMAND FOR
SERVICES AND LONG-TERM
OUTCOMES

BRAIN SCIENCE AND AUTISM

DYNAMIC INTELLIGENCE

SOCIETY: SUPPORT THROUGH
COMMUNITY EDUCATION, EMPOW-
ERMENT, AND RESPONSIBILITY

THE VALUE OF NEURODIVERSITY

for his parents. Donald lacked interest in others (including his parents), lacked desire to interact socially, and had a strong requirement for sameness and ritualistic structure. On the advice of their doctor, Donald's parents institutionalized him at three years old in a sanatorium called the Preventorium.[46]

While other children stayed at the Preventorium for three to six months, Donald did not appear to make progress there; instead, his behavior and skills regressed. He became more withdrawn and less interactive with the world around him. After a year, his parents withdrew him from the sanatorium and went in search of more answers. They found Dr. Leo Kanner, a renowned child psychiatrist who described Donald's symptoms as being similar to schizophrenia—marked by social withdrawal and lack of interest—but could not give a definitive diagnosis. Dr. Kanner tracked Donald for several years, after which he had identified more children with similar behavioral expressions. By 1943, Kanner had identified ten additional children with "autistic disturbance of affective contact" and gave Donald a diagnosis of "autism." Donald was called "Case 1"—the first person to ever be formally diagnosed with autism.[47]

When Donald was eleven, he went to live with a couple on a farm, where his abilities were put to use in activities and duties on the farm. His time on the farm was transformative. After four years, he returned home and attended public high school. At twenty-five years old, he received bachelor's degrees in French and mathematics, going on to work at the bank owned by his family. He was able to learn to drive, has lived alone, and has travelled independently and extensively over the course of his life.

---

46 "Mississippi State Sanatorium Museum," Boswell Regional Center, accessed March 15, 2018, http://www.brc.ms.gov/Pages/Sanatorium.aspx.

47 John Donvan and Caren Zucker, "Donald Grey Triplett: The first boy diagnosed as autistic," *BBC News*, last modified January 21, 2016, http://www.bbc.com/news/magazine-35350880.

Today, Donald Triplett still lives in Forest, Mississippi. He lives in his own house, is an avid golfer, and is a known member of the community, where he is accepted and supported by people who have known him all his life. By all accounts, he has lived a life doctors did not believe he could when he was institutionalized as a boy.

Why is it important to learn about Donald Triplett? This amazing example of the first person diagnosed with autism could easily have been the story of a child committed to an institution and residing there for his entire life. Instead, against so many odds—the social pressure of the times to not be different; the lack of understanding that resulted in children with disabilities being sent away to institutions, some forgotten forever—Donald's life turned out to be extraordinary. Through the perseverance of his parents, going against the pressure and social norms of their times, and through his own determination and hard work, Donald has created a life for himself that has been fulfilling and self-sufficient. In addition, the support and acceptance of his community have kept him safe and taken care of all these years.

How do we achieve these goals—independence, meaningful contribution, and fulfillment—for as many individuals with developmental disorders such as autism as possible, across the globe?

In taking a step back and looking at the autism services industry, what should our goals be? Our goals as investors, providers, clinicians, and members of communities, where now one in sixty-eight individuals are diagnosed with autism, should be to support and empower those individuals to live lives focused on strengths, abilities, social contribution, and personal fulfillment, with as much independence as possible.

To conclude this book, I want to focus on the theme that ties investments, services provisions, clinical work, and communities together: empowerment. This chapter will address how investors, clinicians, providers, and communities can affect the future of autism services and the quality of life autistic individuals will have. Together, they can empower individuals to create and fulfill a joyful vision for their lives.

FAQ:

WHAT ARE SOME OF THE KEY FACTORS AND RISKS INVESTORS SHOULD WEIGH WHEN EXPLORING THE PROVIDER LANDSCAPE?

Attrition: Turnover rates in the autism provider market are generally high. For direct interventionists, the rates are between 40 and 75 percent, and for supervisors, between 5 and 20 percent. The costs associated with recruitment and training, not to mention the disruption to services and customer dissatisfaction as a result, can negatively impact the business's operations and ability to scale.

Fraud: Fraud has been a long-standing issue, but more recently there has been a rise in reported cases of individuals posing as BCBAs and providing "services" by using others' BCBA numbers to illegally bill for services, billing for services that did not occur or for clients who have never been seen by the provider, and billing for services that are unbillable. There is also the issue of unintentional fraud where companies do not understand the regulations regarding billing and are unknowingly billing fraudulently.

Workforce classification: Many providers classify their direct interventionists as independent contractors to cut operational costs while treating them as an employee. Misclassification can result in expensive penalties and creates legal risk for the business.

Lack of clinical quality: While many service providers are providing excellent care, there are a significant portion of companies who are compromising on quality and clinical integrity and, ultimately, on client outcomes. While this may not be the most important consideration for an investor, every day of intervention is an opportunity to move a client's life forward and empower them to create a better future. This is also a differentiator for providers as clinical outcomes determine length of services and other factors that payers are concerned about.

Payer concentration: Many providers have significant payer concentration reliant on either a specific state or federal law.

Revenue model: There are a variety of models in the autism service provider landscape, including:

- In-home services only

- Center-based services only

- School-based services

- Multi-site, multi-service delivery

Brand and reputation: This is a small and fragmented market presenting many opportunities for consolidation and sophistication. Brand and reputation is important, especially when consolidating companies, specifically due to the nature of the ABA market and the types of interventions companies are providing.

Billing and collections: As with other areas of health-care, providers are managing commercial payer denials, billing and collection issues, and documentation com-plexities. Some of these issues are exacerbated in the autism market due to the recent changes in the funding landscape.

INVESTORS: SOCIAL IMPACT THROUGH FINANCIAL INVESTMENT

The field of autism services provides a unique opportunity for investors: a place where their money can both provide a strong return and make a lasting impact. While investors have to be concerned with ROI, not all opportunities come with as much potential for social empowerment. I believe that the world is becoming more conscientious, and more and more investors are looking for ways to have a positive impact.

Why should investors care about outcomes and not just financial returns? The clearest answer is because of autism's growing prevalence and the increasing likelihood that it will affect all of our lives in some way. Without promoting independence and self-sufficiency, the cost to support an autistic individual across his or her lifetime is anywhere between $1.4 and $2.4 million—something society will have to bear.[48] Investors have just as much reason to care about this as anyone else, and they have the resources to help propel a rapidly growing market.

That's why, while this book is geared toward investors, I've included content aimed at providers as well. It's important that investors understand the industry and how they can help shape it in a positive way. Likewise, it is important for providers to understand what private equity can do for the industry. Private equity is interested in this field because there is a healthy, growing market. By working together to provide value, investors and providers can grow the industry and make money while also making a very meaningful impact.

---

48 "Lifetime Costs of Autism Average $1.4 million to $2.4 Million," Autism Speaks, last modified June 9, 2014, https://www.autismspeaks.org/science/science-news/lifetime-costs-autism-average-millions.

This is a national, if not global, opportunity. The United States is a leader on many fronts, including autism research and availability of funding and services. Investors who take a strong role in the industry can lead the way globally to transform lives and create economic opportunities.

FAQ:

WHAT ARE KEY BUSINESS DRIVERS FOR INVESTORS WHEN EVALUATING INVESTMENT OPPORTUNITIES?

Investors examine these key business drivers when evaluating a potential investment opportunity:

- Size of the business

- Financial performance

- Demand for services

- Types of payers and payer concentration

- Revenue model

- Service model strategies

- Demonstrated ability to grow and scale

- Quality of the management team

- Strength of systems and infrastructure

- Organization-wide technology systems

- Cost structure of business

- Ability to recruit and train BCBAs and availability of direct care staff

- Attrition/retention

- Utilization of contracted service hours

- Market concentration and expansion opportunities

However, outcomes and quality are vitally important. Right now, the autism services industry is a hugely fragmented marketplace comprised of many well-intentioned, clinically focused, small-scale businesses providing services but without the ability to scale and manage significant growth from an infrastructure and administrative perspective. The larger players in the market have generally, but not always, done a better job at executing growth, but many forego clinical quality and meaningful long-term outcomes in favor of that growth. Investors see the value and strong returns in this rapidly growing marketplace but may not put enough emphasis on the importance of clinical integrity, adhering to best practices, and long-term quality outcomes.

As a consultant to private equity firms and operating companies in the behavioral healthcare market, I stand with conviction for both profitable business results and return on investment alongside good quality, best practices in both the business and clinical divisions of companies, and meaningful outcomes that translate to quality of life for each individual. Good business enables empowering results and strong results are good for business.

SERVICE PROVIDERS: MEETING THE SHIFTING DEMAND FOR SERVICES AND LONG-TERM OUTCOMES

As we stand back and look at the lifespan—the journey of an individual on the autism spectrum—we see that early intensive intervention comprises only a few years of life. Where is the plan for the rest of their lives? Where is the consideration for what years eighteen through seventy-eight are going to be like?

These are questions and concerns that have emerged from the companies I have evaluated as a consultant, the individuals and families with whom I have spoken, and the countless conferences and events at which I have been present. There is significant focus on the science—the discovery, evidence, and best practices—as there should be. However, there is a myopic viewpoint prevalent throughout the industry and service provider marketplace that doesn't take these long-term questions into consideration. Parents and self-advocates are demanding more.

We have reached an important moment in the field of autism services. Either we will continue with the status quo, accept outcomes that, more often than not, do not serve individuals in the long-term, and allow the industry to be steered by those who do not have the necessary knowledge; or we will come together to expand and improve our services, measures, and outcomes. I am convinced that the current implementation of ABA is not enough; it needs to be innovated, evolved, or augmented to better suit the long-term needs of participants.

Some of the adults with whom I have spoken describe the aversive nature of their ABA intervention experiences. In lesser adverse experiences, there are descriptions from individuals about the stress and pressure of having to learn to function in a neurotypical world, of being misunderstood, and of outcomes being measured purely from a neurotypical viewpoint. The future of autism intervention will either require an expanded and evolved version of the general ABA service model being provided today, or individuals and families will continue to explore options beyond what the current implementation of ABA has to offer.

In the introduction, we discussed how autistic people typically want the same things out of life as anyone else: to have meaningful relationships and the ability to provide for themselves. Yet these quality-of-life factors are never really addressed in autism intervention; providers often fail to view these young children as the adults they will become. This is a significant area in which we need to see improvements.

> *Providers often fail to view these young children as the adults they will become.*

We should all be proud of what this industry has accomplished, yet remain committed to ensuring what we do next is even better. We owe it to the autistic community to relentlessly pursue the best and to continue to improve.

BRAIN SCIENCE AND AUTISM

New understanding of the human brain may hold promising applications for the autistic community. As we have discussed, anxiety drives many behaviors in individuals with autism. It is typical for autistic individuals to fidget or engage in self-stimulatory behavior, like twirling their hands or rocking back and forth. In many of the current ABA programs, the focus has been on eliminating these behaviors, but if we aren't addressing the root cause of that anxiety, we're missing a big piece of the puzzle. Brain science may offer us a solution for that—and possibly more. As we come to better understand the brain, we may find keys to break barriers and better understand processes in the autistic mind.

The brain has two modes of processing. There is the nonconscious mode, which is consistently evaluating threats and reward cues: judgments, biases, intuitions. *Is there a threat in this environment? Is there a reward in this environment?* The other mode is conscious processing, which functions at a much slower rate. Conscious processing is verbal processing and rationality. These can override and rationalize your initial, intuitive, nonconscious decision, so the brain may pick up on cues and determine that something isn't safe, even if you rationalize that you are safe. You will still feel panic, because the nonconscious part of your brain works faster. The neural regulation of the autonomic nervous system affects one's ability to focus and learn and also affects behavior.

Autism comes with heightened sensory sensitivity. We have already discussed how autistic individuals use self-stimulation to cope with anxiety. Many interventions aim to eliminate these behaviors, as they are seen as odd and atypical. Now we are starting to understand the purpose of such behavior and the benefits it provides for the individual. As adults with autism will tell you, the anxiety and stress they experience managing social situations and navigating their environments inhibit much of their adaptive functioning.

A new approach to treating disorders of the brain may offer help to autistic individuals. The concept involves training the brain to respond a specific way. Statistically significant data suggest that you can train your brain and consolidate a new habit. Stress reduction, dietary changes, exercise routines, thinking more positively—with wide application, research suggests that after significant repetition, the brain accepts the new habit as part of its daily routine. An example of this type of cognitive restructuring and subsequent modification of behavioral patterns is the cognitive behavioral intervention package (CBIP), which has well-documented research supporting its efficacy for autism. This and other methods of "brain training" can be extremely beneficial when it comes to reducing stress and anxiety, which could be particularly helpful for individuals living with autism.

By training the brain, a significant reduction in stress, anxiety, and depression can be achieved.[49] But according to brain scientists, this technique can also help autistic individuals in other ways. Essentially, we can train the brains of individuals with autism to better pick up social cues. It's all about understanding the way the brain functions and optimizing it to overcome specific issues. This, some believe, will lead to a type of personalized medicine, such as is happening in cancer treatment, training each person's brain *individually* to reduce stress, reduce depression, or in the case of autistic individuals, pick up on missed social cues, recognize facial expressions, and identify emotions.

If true, this could help individuals with autism more easily form human connections. This is another area where the current ABA service model is often deficient, because the methods used in many ABA-based programs result in rule-based learning that is inflexible and not adaptable to the environment.

Knowing where these deficiencies lay, we can explore different approaches, technologies, and therapies to expand the ABA service model, with the aim of improving outcomes in those areas. Brain

---

49 Evian Gordon, Donna M. Palmer, Helen Liu et al., "Online Cognitive Brain Training Associated with Measurable Improvements in Cognition and Emotional Well-Being," *Technology and Innovation* 15, (2013): 53–62.

science is offering some interesting possibilities, and the market is getting involved to make it a reality.

In addition, there is increasing evidence that by engaging the vagus nerve through slow and regulated breathing, all kinds of physiological processes and resulting emotional issues can be ameliorated, such as inflammation, depression, and anxiety.[50] Studies have shown significant improvements for core domains of brain functioning, including feeling, emotion, and self-regulation in addition to the sub-domains of self-regulation: positivity-negativity bias, resilience, and social skills. The potential applicability of these brain training exercises to autism is considerable.

Other companies, realizing the need to relieve anxiety for individuals with autism, are developing approaches and technology to encourage relaxation. An Australian firm called Neurotech has just raised significant funding to develop a neurofeedback-based headband designed to help children with autism relax. They are calling the device Mente Autism.[51] As brain science continues to develop, and the market finds new ways to apply it, new opportunities will be present for autism providers and their investors to help individuals manage the psychological and emotional aspects of autism.

ABA is a remarkable science, but it only looks at observable behavior. It doesn't deal with the emotional state—what's going on inside. If we can incorporate some of these self-relaxation techniques and technological advances into intervention programs for individuals with autism, we could begin to treat the cause of the

---

50   Ibid.

51   SharpBrains, "Australian neurotech firm raises $4m to develop neurofeedback-based headband aimed at helping kids with autism relax and better engage," last modified October 16, 2017, https://sharpbrains.com/blog/2017/10/16/australian-neurotech-firm-raises-4m-to-develop-neurofeedback-based-headband-aimed-at-helping-kids-with-autism-relax-and-better-engage/.

anxiety rather than just focusing on eliminating its symptoms. And if such techniques can help autistic individuals better pick up social cues, identify emotions, and relate socially, then these individuals may be able to greatly improve their ability to interact with and communicate with others. They could also help manage the anxiety and depression that so many adults struggle with and for which they have inadequate support because of the lack of understanding in the psychiatric and psychotherapeutic professional communities about the needs of individuals with autism.

DYNAMIC INTELLIGENCE

Dynamic intelligence concerns our ability to adapt our thinking to circumstances in order to navigate a complex and hectic world. Individuals with autism are static thinkers—that is, they think linearly and like the stability or structure of a routinized way of living. However, dynamic thinking and problem-solving are fundamental to being able to maintain a job, live independently, and navigate the social world. You need to be able to walk into a room, assess what is happening, and be able to decide how to act. Each set of circumstances will be different, requiring flexibility and adaptation.

As I discussed earlier, Christine, a college graduate, expressed to me that she learned social skills in a social skills group. When she got to college, the students with whom she was trying to engage were not following the "rules" she had learned in her social skills group. It was tough for her to manage the flexibility and problem-solving requirements of those social situations, as they did not follow the scripted interactions that she had learned. This is not an uncommon outcome of many social skills programs.

The majority of current ABA intervention programs do not include dynamic thinking and flexible problem-solving skills in their curricula. Many parents have commented to me that they have gone outside of their ABA program, to programs such as relationship development intervention (RDI), to access support for teaching their children these vital skills. RDI is a family-based, cognitive developmental approach to treating autism that is built on the theory that dynamic intelligence and the ability to think flexibly are critical to functioning. RDI focuses on building a "guided participation" relationship between parents and their child. The objectives of RDI are to teach the autistic child the ability to learn from the subjective experiences of others; the ability to coordinate one's own behaviors to successfully participate socially; the ability to use communication to invite interactions and curiosity and to share feelings; the ability to alter plans as circumstances change; the ability to solve problems that lack clear-cut solutions; and the ability to anticipate what might happen in the future based on past experiences.

Compared to the thousands of studies published from decades of peer-reviewed research evaluating the efficacy of ABA methodology, there is very little scientific evidence to support the efficacy of RDI. The intent of peer review is to have your methodology replicated and evaluated by others working in the same field. A handful of studies have been published examining RDI, mostly conducted by the creator of this technique and his colleagues. One study, published in 2007, reviewed the progress of sixteen children who received RDI services between 2000 and 2005.[52] They examined changes in the scores of these participants on two diagnostic assessment tools for autism. Their review showed that whereas all sixteen children met

---

52 SE Gutstein, AF Burgess, and K Montfort, "Evaluation of the relationship development intervention program," *Autism* 11, no. 5 (September 2007): 397–411, doi:10.1177/1362361307079603.

the diagnostic criteria for autism (on the ADOS and ADI-R) prior to treatment, none of the children met the diagnostic criteria for autism at follow-up. There were many factors in this study that limit the conclusions that can be drawn, such as the lack of a control group or comparison group, as well as how the intervention was conducted. Limited studies showing favorable outcomes have been conducted combining some developmental approaches with ABA programs. More research is needed. A report released in 2010 by the CMS labels RDI an "emerging evidence-based intervention for children with ASD."[53]

As a professional who believes in evidence-based treatments, it is challenging and dissonant for me to recommend to families that they pursue any program that lacks sufficient scientific support. Having said that, parents are reporting that the relatability and flexible problem-solving that RDI and other developmentally focused programs teach is what's missing from our current model of ABA programs.

My friend Julie described to me how their ABA program taught her son the rules of how to clean up after himself after preparing and eating a meal. It was relatively scripted and rule-based, and her son was taught to follow instructions such as "time to clean up." With RDI, she was taught to present situations to him, instead of instructions, and encourage him to practice curiosity and hindsight/foresight (examining what happened in the past and how that can help anticipate what might need to happen in the future) to determine what to do next. So instead of giving him an instruction to clean up after a meal, she would say things like, "What a great meal! Look at the countertop," and engage flexible thinking to get him to recognize

---

53 Julie Young, Carolyn Corea, James Kimani, and David Mandell, "Autism Spectrum Disorders (ASDs) Services: Final Report on Environmental Scan," Centers for Medicare and Medicaid Services, last modified March 9, 2010, https://www.medicaid.gov/medicaid/ltss/downloads/autism-spectrum-disorders.pdf.

that the areas where he had prepared food needed to be cleared off and cleaned up. This expanded to walking into a room and helping him assess who was there, who was talking to whom, and whether it would be appropriate to interject into a conversation to stand by and listen. The goal is to become comfortable with "expecting the unexpected" and learn how to create states of connection between them and others.

The question is, can I invite ABA service providers to meet this important developmental need using our science and methodology, or will families be forced to look outside of ABA programs to gain this support? I know a few ABA providers who are blending developmental and ABA programs together, but not all funding sources support this approach because of the lack of sufficient evidence. It's time the ABA community of providers rethinks how it is teaching social skills and problem-solving. Too many adults are sharing how they lack the skills to integrate and manage socially, which prevents employment, independent living, intimate relationships, friendships, and safe community integration.

SOCIETY: SUPPORT THROUGH COMMUNITY EDUCATION, EMPOWERMENT, AND RESPONSIBILITY

As we work to evolve and improve our industry and services, we must also focus on fostering a better understanding of autism and the needs of those living with autism in the community. Through educating the community, we can breed acceptance and compassion. We can help make the world a little more inviting to individuals with autism and, in turn, our communities will be better for it.

Think about Don Triplett and what we can learn from his story. It shares a common theme I have heard from many self-advocates about how crucial it was for them to have parents who accepted who they were and helped them function in society. Having parents devoted to helping them build on their strengths seems to be a key component in these individuals' ability to thrive.

One young woman told me at a conference that doctors had advised her parents to institutionalize her when she was a baby. Today, she works for a big corporation, she's married, and she's expecting a baby. Because her parents decided not to place her in an institution and worked to ensure that she learned and grew as a person, she has gone on to live a rewarding and successful life. She's not alone, either. I have come to know many people who have gone on to live very independent lives, led successful careers, and forged meaningful relationships, because their parents and their community focused on nurturing and celebrating their strengths.

Stephen Shore is another such individual. We talked about Shore earlier, a professor who travels the world educating people about autism and the needs of the autistic community. He too credits his parents for much of his success. Rather than taking the advice of doctors and institutionalizing him, Shore's parents used music and many different types of interventions to help him. This was many years before the early intervention movement. Thanks to the support of his parents, Shore evaded institutionalization and, subsequently, has gone on to live a successful and fulfilling life.

This supportive approach to parenting of autistic children can be facilitated through community understanding. The more knowledge the community has about autism and the needs of those living with it, the more support individuals with autism receive, and the more knowledge future parents of children with autism will possess. More emphasis should be placed on educating the public about autism and teaching people proper etiquette for interacting with autistic individuals.

Conversely, when we fail to teach the community about autism and instill proper etiquette, the results are a lack of understanding and often a lack of compassion. Investigations suggest that anywhere from 40 to 75 percent of children with autism experience bullying and that teachers often fail to intervene.[54] This can lead to debilitating mental health and self-esteem issues. Such discouragement can be destructive and prohibitive regarding individuals with autism being able to realize their potential.

Of course, etiquette goes further than just not bullying people. Author and self-advocate Russell Lehmann recently detailed how, while flying to give a talk, flight delays and missed flight connections pushed him to the edge of his tolerance level, and he succumbed to an overwhelming meltdown. He was lying on the floor behind a ticket counter at the airport and was overcome with convulsions and uncontrollable crying; Lehmann was unable to calm himself down. An American Airlines employee found him and comforted him, supported him through his episode, made sure he got on a plane, and helped get him to his destination. The compassion and understanding demonstrated by that American Airlines employee made a huge difference for Russell.

There was a similar story in the news recently, where a young boy was having a meltdown on a plane. A woman on the plane took the boy into the galley and helped him calm down. These stories underscore the importance of educating the community about how

---

54 Connie Anderson, "IAN Research Report: Bullying and Children with ASD," Interactive Autism Network, last modified October 7, 2014, https://iancommunity.org/cs/ian_research_reports/ian_research_report_bullying.

to reach out to individuals with autism and understand what's going on and what they are experiencing. The community has to learn to embrace the differences and not ostracize these individuals. Through education, understanding can be gained and compassion grown. Individuals with autism need help to interact and communicate, but the community also needs to embrace, accept, and empathize with them.

An educated community is a thoughtful community—one that will reach out to and support individuals who need it. An educated community will allow parents to feel stronger and more supported in their efforts and will give them an opportunity to become engaged in the community instead of remaining secluded at home. It will create teachers and employers who will better understand individuals with autism and their needs.

When the community isn't educated, disaster can happen. There are too many stories with disastrous outcomes, both for caregivers of individuals with autism and for the autistic individuals themselves, when traditional protocols are applied to situations without taking into consideration the needs and sensitivities of autistic individuals. I recently read a story in the news about a young man with autism who took his own life. A typical evening turned into a nightmare when the young man reportedly became upset after a phone call with his former girlfriend. He came home and was holed up in his room with a gun and his dog. He asked to be left alone to calm down. In the meantime, the police were called to check on his welfare. The police check and a series of phone calls led to the parents being removed from the home and the SWAT team being called in along with dozens of police officers. They broke windows in the house and put cameras inside to see what he was doing. The parents begged the police to leave him alone and to let him decompress, but they continued to do what SWAT teams do when they think someone is at risk. Sadly, he ended up shooting himself. The young man's father believes the incident was preventable—that the police's intimidating show of force turned this situation into something much worse than it was and created a life or death scenario.

This is but one example of many where law enforcement and first responders have escalated situations unnecessarily, because the behavior of an autistic individual has been misunderstood. Just search online and you will see the prevalence. Tragically, police and first responder interactions with autistic individuals too often result in trauma or harm to the autistic individual and even their caregivers.

Thankfully, over the past twenty-five years, the community in general has become a lot more knowledgeable. But tragedies like this are a sign that there is still a long way to go and a lot of ignorance to combat. Had the police understood autism better—had they paused to listen—there is a good chance that there would have been a different outcome to this story.

Community education must play a vital role in the autism industry moving forward. It will better prepare future parents of autistic children, as well as the children's teachers, peers, and employers. It can foster better practices among teachers and care-givers, and it will breed understanding, compassion, and support among the greater population, ultimately creating a friendlier and more inviting society for individuals living on the spectrum.

To this end, organizations like the Autism Society Los Angeles (ASLA) and others across the country are working hard to make a change. To date, ASLA has trained over five thousand police officers in Los Angeles about autism in an effort to prevent unnecessary arrests and tragedies. Community support of such efforts will go a long way in spreading awareness of this vital issue.

THE VALUE OF NEURODIVERSITY

When our communities are more understanding and supportive of individuals with autism, they will be able to more easily share their gifts with us. There is an innate social value in having individuals who see the world from different perspectives. Neurodiversity means we also have a diversity of ideas and new approaches available to us. This is a fact that markets are already embracing, as we see more and more companies focusing energy on bringing individuals with autism into their fold.

Recently, large corporations such as SAP, Hewlett-Packard Enterprise, Microsoft, Ford, Dell Technologies, Deloitte, IBM, and others have launched specific efforts to capitalize on the unique gifts and talents offered by autistic individuals. They have reformed their human resource processes and engaged specifically trained individuals to support the needs of these employees and make the workplace accommodations required to enhance their engagement and productivity. These organizations are leveraging specific skills in areas such as music, mathematics, and pattern recognition, resulting in multiple benefits, both internally and externally. Companies report that this viewpoint of neurodiversity as a competitive advantage is increasing productivity, improving quality, enhancing company reputation, boosting innovation, and improving employee engagement.[55]

Autistic individuals often have trouble getting past the interview stage of a job application or maintaining a job because of their lacking social skills, eccentricities, blatant honesty, and sensory intolerance for environmental factors such as auditory or visual overstim-

---

55 S. Silberman, *Neurotribes: The Legacy of Autism and Future of Neurodiversity* (New York: Penguin, 2015), 483; Robert D. Austin and Gary P. Pisano, "Neurodiversity as a Competitive Advantage," *Harvard Business Review* (May–June 2017), https://hbr.org/2017/05/neurodiversity-as-a-competitive-advantage.

ulation. Understanding these aspects of their wiring and function and modifying the environment to support them, such as giving an employee headphones to reduce auditory stimulations, allows employers to benefit from the unique talents of autistic individuals and enables them to contribute.

When I visited the Israeli Defense Force (IDF) and other programs in Israel, we saw autistic individuals working in different areas of the army, such as laundry service and high-speed data entry and analysis. Being able to participate in the army alongside all their peers was critical to their self-esteem and helped develop many independent living skills. In addition, the IDF and other organizations were able to utilize exceptional skills, such as the ability to analyze aerial and satellite imagery due to their pattern-recognition abilities, or the performance of high-speed, real-time data input while watching live video streams of activity and passenger behavior at train stations.

The typical recruitment process and requirements of most companies would screen out individuals with autism and other disabilities early on. When we consider the standard criteria that make up a "good employee"—competent (does the employee have the necessary verbal and social skills, experience, and education?), capable (is the employee able to do what the job requires and more?), and compatible (does this employee get along well with others?)— your typical autistic person would not fare well during the screening or, if they make it through screening, the interview process. This calls for innovation and forward thinking about how to recruit and interview employees so that a broader pool of talent can be accessed. As companies look to innovate and compete in today's environment, they need employees who see the world in unique and different ways.

This presents new opportunities for entrepreneurs and organizations such as Specialisterne, a software company founded in 2004 by

Thorkil Sonne, who hires neurodiverse talent and developed non-interview methods for assessing and developing the skills of autistic employees. Specialisterne focuses on the high motivation, exceptional ability to focus, persistence, and high learning ability of autistic individuals. Sonne calls his employees "specialists" and capitalizes on their precision, attention to detail, desire for structure, and patient acceptance of repetitive tasks, which are relevant in the technology and software development field. Sonne modifies work environments and office culture to match the sensory sensitivities of his employees. When companies begin work with Specialisterne, they are educated about autism and the needs of autistic individuals in terms of communication style and social interaction, and companies have reported improvements in their internal communication based on the modifications they have had to make to communicate clearly with autistic software support specialists. Specialisterne boasts higher performance and a lower fault rate in data conversion than their competitors.[56]

Whether in national defense or on the frontlines of technology, a neurodiverse team will be able to excel in ways a neurotypical team would not. By capitalizing on the unique perspectives of individuals with autism, companies and governments can find new approaches to solve problems and unlock new paths of innovation. But first, employers and the community at large must learn of the value of neurodiversity and how traditional employment screening effectively pushes many autistic individuals out of the workforce. Only when we create a world that is understanding and accepting of neurodiversity will we receive the economic, social, scientific, and technological benefits that neurodiversity can achieve.

---

56 "Thorkil Sonne," Ashoka.org, https://www.ashoka.org/en/fellow/thorkil-sonne.

INSPIRED ACTION

F rom where I stand, it is clear that the autism services industry needs to jump an S-curve. Now that I have been able to evaluate the industry without the personal attachment to my business, I have a more objective perspective.

Many of the issues with autism services are simply related to the ego of the industry. Until we are ready to collaborate and agree upon multiple variables such as outcome measurements and share data, we aren't going to be able to ask the important questions, like "Where are we helping the most?" and "What's missing?" Perhaps the current autism intervention models can only teach 60 percent of what these individuals need to live full lives, which means the ABA service delivery model needs to be expanded or evolved. Or perhaps we have the technology but are just focusing on the wrong things. But we are not going to be able to properly move forward if we cannot accurately assess our current strengths and weaknesses.

Stepping back has also allowed me to more clearly see inherent problems with the notion of normalization—the idea that individuals with autism have to be fixed. When I first entered the industry, the phrase "indistinguishable from their peers" was the goal of intervention. Treatment programs operated on a Lovaas-driven model of intensive, mostly adult-directed interventions on the premise that you could make a child with autism look and behave "normally"—indistinguishably from their peers—essentially "recovering" them from their autism and forcing them to be someone they're not. Some providers still promote this goal, but most individuals with autism and their families disagree with the use of the term "recovery." It implies an illness that needs to be healed. What I hear most is the desire for awareness, understanding, and acceptance.

It also perpetuates the idea that autism can be cured. That instills harmful notions in the minds of children with autism and sets unrealistic expectations for their parents or caregivers. Likewise, it exacerbates societal perceptions that isolate and ostracize people with autism. It's time for the industry to face reality; to assess where we are with real, long-term, standardized outcomes; and to drop the notion that any of these people need to be, or should be, fixed.

Rather, we should be focusing on how best to teach them the skills they need to have full lives and be participatory in the world around them instead of the denials for jobs, choice, opportunity, support, and quality of life that is the daily experience of most individuals. Society can benefit greatly from the wealth of contributions that come from autistic individuals.

As an industry, I believe we have reached a crucial moment. Intense investor interest, combined with greater funding availability, can bring tremendous growth to autism services. However, it is incumbent upon us to make sure that growth is wise and that we also progress our vision and strengthen our services to build great futures for individuals with autism.

With conscious investment, progressive clinical approaches, services aimed at long-term quality of life goals, and educated communities, we can empower autistic individuals, grow the market, provide a wealth of business opportunities, and make lasting and significant social change—the type of change that will invite social contributions from a neurologically diverse population of individuals who see the world in ways we do not.

I believe that all of us should care about creating the best possible futures for individuals with autism. It is a mission with great social and financial benefit. If we do not, we will all bear the economic and human cost of not doing so. It is our collective responsibility to support autistic individuals in obtaining what they need to live as independent a life as possible and pave the way for them to become self-determined citizens of the world.

AFTERWORD

"I run Autism Spectrum Therapies. Our purpose is to advance outcomes for autistic individuals. I have over seven hundred staff, six hundred of whom are behavior interventionists. We drive to our customers. Not an easy business model, but I know it is best for our clients. Our primary source of revenue, the state of California, is preparing to announce a big retroactive rate cut and has not paid us for many months. We need to quickly and dramatically reorganize and rewrite our clinical program to maintain quality and individualization of interventions while operating with a margin. I need to move fast. Can you help?"

Dr. Ronit Molko said this to me in the spring of 2010. What was curious to me at the time was her matter-of-fact description of her circumstance and clear intention to muscle through the changes that needed to happen. What was not clear to me was if Ronit fully understood how dire her circumstances were. Having driven large scale corporate change for decades, I had first-hand knowledge that nine out of ten companies and leaders facing similar circumstances failed during these whole-system transformations. Ronit was either uninformed, fool-hearted, or acting with rare and enrolling courage. I had to find out, so I agreed to help with the turnaround. After all, her mission was compelling.

What neither of us knew at the time was that the business environment was about to get worse, much worse. In 2012, another wave of change would force Ronit and Autism Spectrum Therapies (AST) to pivot their funding stream completely. Insurance companies, instead of the state of California, would become their first line of funding. Within two years, half of AST's invoices would be going to a completely new payee. Ronit was not facing just one mandate to "jump the S-curve, which is difficult for any leader; she was going to be forced to jump two S-curves in less than forty-eight months.

Back in 2010, most in Ronit's trusted inner circle advised her to close AST down and cut her losses. If I was clear headed, perhaps I would have advised the same. But there was something about Ronit that enrolled me in this noble and mighty effort and I was not alone in choosing to stand with her. Most of Ronit's leadership team stayed with her from beginning to end of AST's transformation.

Over the next several years, much changed inside AST. But Ronit's unwillingness to compromise in the quality of care that AST provided their customers and her relentless pursuit of more effective methods never changed. Her pursuit began with the publication of her dissertation in 1999 and the publication of *Autism Matters* shows she is not letting up soon.

What makes this book so valuable to those wanting to better understand the business and consumer sides of autism therapies is that, in addition to being a recognized expert on the clinical models, Ronit launched and scaled a world-class services company that provided therapies to thousands of customers and led her company through multiple existential threats. This required her to demonstrate a mastery of operations, finances, human resources, and state and insurance bureaucracies. I distinctively remember multiple times when Ronit would get in her car to pick up payment checks in person to save a few days. Ronit was the triple threat leader who was willing to persist variously and do whatever it took—a rare commodity in my experience.

One of the keys to the successful transformation of AST was Ronit's willingness to grow personally and professionally. Ronit is formidable, having been forged in fire. Once righted in the new market realities and set up for sustainable and profitable growth, Ronit led AST through its acquisition by Learn It Systems. Once again, she learned what she needed and did what was required to negotiate effectively in the realm of mergers and acquisitions. Having helped in successfully integrating the companies post acquisition, I and others encouraged Ronit to step back and consolidate her insights and compose her thoughts.

The result is what you are holding now in your hands. In *Autism Matters*, Ronit shares from her head the science and facts around individuals with autism and the most effective ways companies can serve them. She shares from her business experience how to build a business that does good while growing profitably. She shares from her heart the hope that, with the number of people with autism growing, businesses will grow in capability and capacity to outfit them with what they need to be as independent as possible, make positive contributions to society, and lead self-determined lives.

Chris McGoff

Author, Speaker, Founder of The Clearing Inc.

THE POWER OF ABA: TWO STORIES FROM MY TIME IN THE FIELD AS AN ABA THERAPIST

The first child I was assigned to work with lived in a mobile home, thirty minutes outside of Lawrence, Kansas, down a long, sandy road. Her familial circumstances were challenging, and her only caretaker, a male relative, was not very interested in learning about her treatment, nor about the ins and outs of ABA. This young girl, about seven years old, did not have any verbal communicative skills and exhibited pica—the persistent eating of substances that contain no nutritional value. She ate items such as batteries, fabrics, dirt, and drywall. Her pica was so severe that everything had been removed

TOPICS AHEAD:

THE POWER OF ABA: TWO STORIES FROM MY TIME IN THE FIELD AS AN ABA THERAPIST

A BRIEF HISTORY LESSON ON APPLIED BEHAVIOR ANALYSIS (ABA)

THE STORY OF DICKY

THE HISTORY OF THE LANTERMAN ACT

EVIDENCE-BASED & NON-EVIDENCE BASED INTERVENTIONS FOR AUTISM from her bedroom except a metal cot for her to sleep on. Everything in this home was padlocked, and if left unsupervised for a moment, she would try to get her hands on whatever she could ingest.

I was completely overwhelmed by the responsibility of working directly with this young girl and her caregiver. Fortunately, I had the support and guidance of a number of professionals, who helped me navigate the intervention program with this family. We implemented a basic picture communication system for her, which gave her some elementary communication tools for the first time in her life. A medical evaluation helped rule out nutritional deficiencies that often cause the craving for inedible items associated with pica, and a behavioral program including antecedent strategies (modification of the environment), overcorrection (repeating a behavior to reduce the occurrence of inappropriate of self-injurious behaviors), and differential reinforcement (reinforcing only the desired response and ignoring other responses) was put in place.

In addition, we recommended occupational therapy to help her with sensory reinforcement, so her sensory needs could be met another way. By the time our funding stopped, she was no longer engaging in pica and was able to have a mattress and blankets back in her room, along with some basic furniture and toys. I have never forgotten this young girl and often wonder what became of her. This experience gave me a very different perspective into how families in very remote and rural areas, who typically are not able to access services easily, are managing (or not managing) the challenges they face raising children with autism and other special needs.

The second young girl I worked with was in her early teens. She also lived in a small trailer with her mother, stepfather, and two siblings, but this family lived in a community. Our program focused on activities of daily living, as her parents needed support getting her ready for school and helping her transition at the end of the day. Her stepfather was prone to angry outbursts, and on more than one occasion I arrived at the home to find him in a rage, once even waving a gun in the air while yelling at his family. Interestingly, it was not that simple to get Child Protective Services to step in. Because we were already in the home working on parent education and support, the state was looking at us to mitigate the situation.

As the goals of her program were focused on getting her ready for school, I was assigned to work with her from 5:30 a.m. until 7 a.m., when the bus picked her up, and from 4:45 p.m. until 7:30 p.m. after school, three days a week. Having never lived in a cold climate, this was quite the experience for me. Living in Kansas in the winter was one thing. Having to go outside at 5 a.m. to turn on my car in 15° F temperatures so it could defrost for fifteen minutes before I had to leave for work was quite another. And then trying to cajole a teen out of bed in those frigid temperatures (their mobile home was not well-heated) and prompt her through her morning schedule of dressing, tooth brushing, hair brushing, preparing and eating breakfast, packing her backpack, and waiting with her for the bus to arrive, all without an outburst or meltdown, was no effortless task.

I learned a great deal from her and the stress that her family was experiencing. I used what I had learned from my days at the traumatic brain injury facility, watching unsuspecting residents being woken from bed in winter and put in cold showers. I brought a hot water bottle with me every morning and placed it on her as I woke her up. This way I could coax her out of bed with something warm to hold while she dressed herself. I used visual schedules and other behavioral strategies so she could anticipate and understand what her morning routine consisted of, and timers to help her manage her time for each task.

What I learned the most from her was the importance of individualizing the program to meet not only the needs of the individual but also the needs of the family. This family was experiencing extreme stress. Examining and assessing her needs within the context of the family's routines, needs, and capacities helped us not only give her many self-management and independence skills but also helped the family manage their stress.

A BRIEF HISTORY LESSON ON APPLIED BEHAVIOR ANALYSIS (ABA)

EXPERIMENTAL PSYCHOLOGY

John B. Watson published *Psychology as the Behaviorist Views It* in 1913. Watson proposed that observable behavior, and not states of mind or mental processes (such as those argued by Sigmund Freud), should be the targeted subject matter for study in psychology.

B.F. Skinner published *The Behavior of Organisms* in 1938. The study formally launched the experimental branch of behavior analysis. Skinner defined two types of behavior: *respondent* and *operant*.

Respondent behavior is reflexive and involuntary. Ivan Pavlov, in his research with dogs, discovered that a neutral stimulus, such as a bell, could be associated with an unconditioned stimulus (food), ultimately leading to the neutral stimulus becoming a conditioned stimulus leading to a conditioned response (salivation).

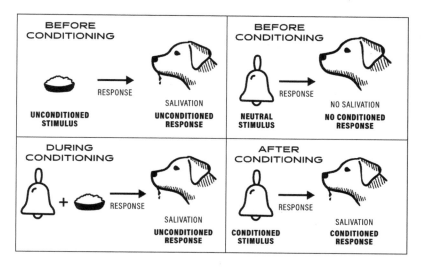

Operant behavior is shaped by what happens *after* a behavior occurs, that is, the consequence of behaviors.

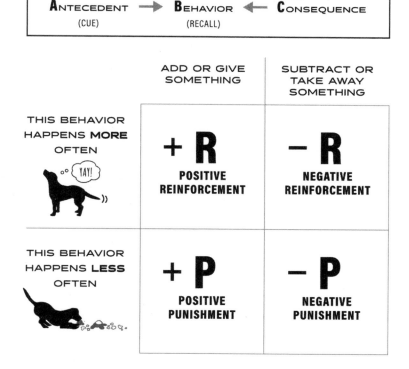

Through thousands of experiments, Skinner systematically manipulated stimuli preceding and following behavior and discovered the basic principles of operant behavior. This established the foundation for behavior analysis as we know it today.

During the 1950s and 60s, researchers used the experimental analysis of behavior to determine whether the principles of behavior conditioning demonstrated in the lab with animals (typically rats and pigeons), could be replicated with humans. Teodoro Ayllon, Jack Michael, Sidney Bijou,[57] Donald Baer,[58] Montrose Wolf, Todd Risley, and others studied several principles of behavior with both typically developing individuals and those with intellectual disabilities. By studying the effects of punishment, escape, and avoidance contingencies, the effects of operant conditioning, as well as other systematic studies of the principles of behavior, these early researchers established the applicability of the principles of behavior to humans and set the stage for ABA.[59]

57 Sidney W. Bijou, "Patterns of Reinforcement and Resistance to Extinction in Young Children," *Child Development* 28, no. 1 (March 1957): 47-54.

58 Sideny W. Bijou and Donald M. Baer, "*A systematic and empirical theory,*" *Child Development* 1, (1961).

59 Sidney W. Bijou et al., "Programmed Instruction as an Approach to Teaching of Reading, Writing, and Arithmetic to Retarded Children," *The Psychological Record* 16, no. 4 (October 1966): 505-22.

Wolf, Risley, and Mees authored a paper[60] in 1964 that describes one of the formative attempts to apply behavioral procedures to the challenging behaviors exhibited by an autistic child, Dicky, who also refused to wear his glasses and risked losing much of his vision. Behavioral procedures were effectively used with Dicky to reduce multiple maladaptive behaviors and establish the consistent wearing of his glasses. He successfully graduated high school.

Baer, Wolf, and Risley published a seminal paper[61] in 1968 outlining the principles of ABA and defining the criteria for judging the adequacy of research and practice in ABA. This paper is still used today as the standard description of ABA and these principles guide the evaluation of best practices in programs.

Ivar Lovaas made significant contributions in 1973 and 1987. Lovaas introduced behaviorally based approaches to treatment, reinforcing "appropriate" behavior and discouraging or punishing inappropriate and self-injurious behaviors. Lovaas constructed a model of intervention for children with autism involving intensive intervention and demonstrated significant improvements in their levels of functioning. This led to the development of the EIBI—early intensive behavior intervention—program and launched the initial intensive treatment program model design for early intervention.

THE STORY OF DICKY

The experimental analysis of behavior produced several powerful techniques for altering and managing behavior. Most of these experi-

---

60 Montrose M. Wolf, Todd Risley, and Hayden Mees, "Application of operant conditioning procedures to the behavioral problems of an autistic child," *Behaviour Research and Therapy* 1, no. 2-4 (1964): 305-12.

61 Donald M. Baer, Montrose M. Wolf, and Todd R. Risley, "Some current dimensions of applied behavioral analysis," *Journal of Applied Behavioral Analysis* 1, no. 1 (1968): 91-7.

ments were conducted by Skinner and his associates with animals in laboratories.

In the 1960s, these techniques were increasingly applied to humans, beginning the experimentation with what would become ABA.

The case study of Dicky, a three-year-old boy who was recovering from a cataract surgery and resided in a psychiatric hospital, was one of the first attempts to apply these techniques and strategies to drastically improve the quality of an individual's life. Dicky refused to wear his glasses, without which he risked losing his eyesight. He displayed temper tantrums and severe self-injury, had sleeping problems and eating difficulties, and lacked typical social and communicative repertoires.

Montrose Wolf developed many techniques to manage Dicky's tantrums, sleeping and eating problems, as well as to establish basic functional communication and socialization, and the wearing of his glasses. After many months of work with Dicky and his family, he successfully returned home to live with his parents. He wore his glasses without issue, his tantrums and sleeping problems were eliminated, and he was learning to communicate verbally and interact socially.

The development of the techniques used to teach Dicky these critical social and functional skills and behaviors is the premier study of dramatically altering behavior and making socially significant changes in an individual's life and resulted in the development of many ABA strategies. Wolf's emphasis on the entirety of a person's life—analyzing consequences, building skills, motivating effort, positivity and enthusiasm, and the focus on social validity—led to the development of other interventions and formed much of the foundation of the principles of ABA.[62]

---

62   Montrose M. Wolf, Todd Risley, and Hayden Mees, "Application of operant conditioning procedures to the behavioral problems of an autistic child," Behaviour Research and Therapy 1, no. 2-4 (1964): 305-12.

HISTORY OF THE LANTERMAN ACT[63]

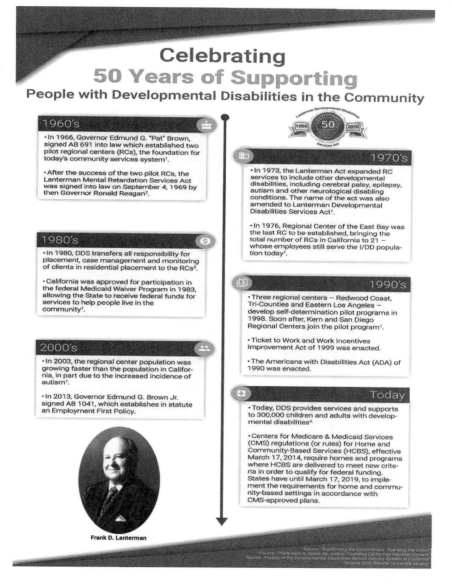

Celebrating
50 Years of Supporting
People with Developmental Disabilities in the Community

1960's
- In 1966, Governor Edmund G. "Pat" Brown, signed AB 691 into law which established two pilot regional centers (RCs), the foundation for today's community services system[1].

- After the success of the two pilot RCs, the Lanterman Mental Retardation Services Act was signed into law on September 4, 1969 by then Governor Ronald Reagan[2].

1970's
- In 1973, the Lanterman Act expanded RC services to include other developmental disabilities, including cerebral palsy, epilepsy, autism and other neurological disabling conditions. The name of the act was also amended to Lanterman Developmental Disabilities Services Act[1].

- In 1976, Regional Center of the East Bay was the last RC to be established, bringing the total number of RCs in California to 21 – whose employees still serve the I/DD population today[1].

1980's
- In 1980, DDS transfers all responsibility for placement, case management and monitoring of clients in residential placement to the RCs[3].

- California was approved for participation in the federal Medicaid Waiver Program in 1983, allowing the State to receive federal funds for services to help people live in the community[1].

1990's
- Three regional centers – Redwood Coast, Tri-Counties and Eastern Los Angeles – develop self-determination pilot programs in 1998. Soon after, Kern and San Diego Regional Centers join the pilot program[1].

- Ticket to Work and Work Incentives Improvement Act of 1999 was enacted.

- The Americans with Disabilities Act (ADA) of 1990 was enacted.

2000's
- In 2003, the regional center population was growing faster than the population in California, in part due to the increased incidence of autism[1].

- In 2013, Governor Edmund G. Brown Jr. signed AB 1041, which establishes in statute an Employment First Policy.

Today
- Today, DDS provides services and supports to 300,000 children and adults with developmental disabilities[4].

- Centers for Medicare & Medicaid Services (CMS) regulations (or rules) for Home and Community-Based Services (HCBS), effective March 17, 2014, require homes and programs where HCBS are delivered to meet new criteria in order to qualify for federal funding. States have until March 17, 2019, to implement the requirements for home and community-based settings in accordance with CMS-approved plans.

Frank D. Lanterman

Source: "Reaffirming the Commitment: Realizing the Vision"
Source: "We're Here to Speak for Justice: Founding California's Regional Centers"
Source: "History of the Developmental Disabilities Service Delivery System in California"
Source: "DDS Website (www.dds.ca.gov)"

63 "50th Anniversary Celebration of the Community Services System," State of California Department of Developmental Services, last modified March 2, 2018, http://www.dds.ca.gov/LantermanAct50thAnniversary/.

EVIDENCE-BASED & NON-EVIDENCE-BASED INTERVENTIONS FOR AUTISM

INTERVENTION	DESCRIPTION	COMMENTS + EXAMPLES
ESTABLISHED INTERVENTIONS: (Sufficient evidence is available to determine with confidence that an intervention results in effective outcomes)		
BEHAVIORAL INTERVENTIONS* * The Behavioral Intervention category consists of programs that combine a number of elements together with a behavior reduction or skill acquisition procedure, whereas the remaining established interventions consist of a single procedure or a combination of two elements that comprise the intervention.	These interventions include both antecedent (the modification of events that precede the behavior that is targeted for modification) and consequent (making changes to the environment following the occurrence of the behavior targeted for change) interventions. Examples of targeted skills are: improving motor, cognitive, communication, academic, and play skills, self-regulation and self-management; decreasing disregulation, maladaptive behaviors, nonfunctional patterns of behavior. The programs combine a number of elements together in a procedure. For example, combining modeling and PRT and schedules which is why they are in this category.	This is the largest category of intervention established by the research as demonstrating efficacy and clinical utility. Many research studies conducted by a diverse group of investigators has demonstrated and replicated significant effectiveness. These strategies are based on the principles and methodologies of applied behavior analysis (ABA) and combines multiple procedures into an intervention.

| COGNITIVE BEHAVIORAL INTERVENTION PACKAGE (CBIP) | CBIP involves cognitive restructuring in which the therapist assists the individual in changing distorted patterns of thinking and maladaptive belief systems in relation to the individual's behaviors. For example, the therapist assists the individual in changing "all or nothing thinking," catastrophising, or personalization ("this is all my fault"). CBIP programs that qualify as established interventions have been modified specifically to meet the needs of individuals with autism. | With the addition of recent scientific evidence, CBIP has been moved from an emerging intervention to an established intervention. CBIP has long been an evidence-based, effective treatment package for anxiety and depression. |

INTERVENTION	DESCRIPTION	COMMENTS + EXAMPLES
COMPREHENSIVE BEHAVIORAL TREATMENT FOR YOUNG CHILDREN (CBTYC)	CBTYC programs involve intensive early behavioral interventions targeting a broad range of critical skills and deficits associated with autism spectrum disorder (ASD). Programs target language and communication, social, play, cognitive, interpersonal, motor, maladaptive behaviors, self-help, and self-management skills. Service delivery is intensive (typically twenty-five to forty hours per week for two to three years) provided in-home, at school, and in community settings and programmatic decisions are data-based. Interventions consist of multiple teaching techniques and strategies. See RonitMolko.com for more information	There is abundant research to support the efficacy and clinical utility of these programs. The techniques and strategies employed in these programs are based on the principles of ABA. These programs are widely funded for autism. Discrete trial training (DTT) is often misunderstood because some people think of all ABA intervention as being DTT. DTT is actually one teaching technique within ABA. DTT is a very structured method of adult-directed teaching which uses mass trial instruction to teach a new response or skill. The contingencies are very clear and a reinforcer is presented to strengthen the correct response. Typically, DTT is taught in a structured environment, with the therapist and child sitting opposite each other with a table next to them or between them. DTT breaks down skills into small, "discrete" components and teaches them one by one. For an example of DTT, please go to RonitMolko.com

LANGUAGE TRAINING (PRODUCTION)	This intervention teaches the functional use of spoken words through the use of modeling verbalizations, prompting procedures, and the use of music to teach language and reinforcement for targeted verbal responses. Language training (production) has moved to the established intervention category with the addition of three new studies.	The intervention is naturalistic and uses actual objects, modeling, and natural reinforcers (if the child requests "milk" he gets milk) and capitalizes on preferred objects and activities to teach language.
MODELING	Modeling is the direct demonstration of the target behavior for the participant. For example, if the target behavior is for the child to sit at a desk while in his classroom, watching a video demonstrating how to sit at the desk may help him understand what the expected behavior looks like. This can be applied to a vast array of skills and behaviors.	Modeling is a highly useful technique because anyone can serve as a model; peers, parents, caregivers, and the participant himself can be the model in the video. With today's technology, making videos is easy and quick and, given the affinity of children and adolescents for watching and using technology, it can be a highly engaging and effective teaching tool.

NATURALISTIC TEACHING STRATEGIES (NTS)	Naturalistic Teaching Strategies are a group of strategies used to teach children skills in their natural environment, typically the home, school, and community. Naturally occurring objects and activities in the environment are used for teaching and reinforcement, and these techniques are primarily child-directed, meaning that the therapist follows the child's lead and motivation when selecting activities and objects.	One of the critical components of these programs is the focus on child-directed activities and interests, as well as using objects and activities that the child is likely to encounter regularly in their natural environment. Teaching sessions are loosely structured and vary based on the child's interests that day but embed all the teaching and targeted skills into those interests. An example of an NTS is the natural language paradigm (NLP). For a description of NLP, please see RonitMolko.com

INTERVENTION	DESCRIPTION	COMMENTS + EXAMPLES
PARENT TRAINING	Newly approved as an established intervention, the parent training package focuses on elements of interventions used in studies where parents acted as the therapist or were trained to implement specific strategies. Parents are taught strategies to increase engagement and communication with their child, develop imitation skills, increase joint attention, develop healthy sleep routines, and increase appropriate play.	Parent-delivered interventions can be highly effective and are a very important component of interventions. Parent delivery is especially relevant in areas where services are not readily accessible.
PEER TRAINING PACKAGE	These programs target children aged three to fourteen and focus on teaching peers how to interact with children with autism during social interactions. Peers are trained on how to initiate and respond during social opportunities. The programs are used in school and community settings and can be used during play dates in the home.	One of the core issues for children on the spectrum is difficulty forming friendships and interacting socially, resulting in isolation and loneliness. By teaching peers how to initiate, respond, and interact with children on the spectrum, the likelihood of relationships forming is increased. These programs help children with autism be included socially during lunch, recess, and other activities at school, for example.
PIVOTAL RESPONSE TREATMENT® (PRT)	Pivotal Response Treatment® is a naturalistic intervention model derived from ABA approaches. Rather than target individual behaviors one at a time, PRT® targets pivotal areas of a child's development, such as motivation, responsivity to multiple cues, self-management, and social initiations. The intervention includes motivational procedures such as child choice, task variation, acquisitioning tasks, interspersing maintenance, rewarding attempts, and natural reinforcements.	PRT® is widely researched and has strong evidence to support its efficacy and clinical utility. Parent involvement is key to the delivery of PRT®, as is implementation of the program in the natural environment. PRT® aims to move children with autism towards a more typical developmental trajectory, based on individualized intervention objectives aligned with the specific child's needs. For more information on recent PRT® research and results please visit RonitMolko.com

SCHEDULES	A schedule is a visual aid identifying the activities that are to be completed in a specific period of time and the order in which the activities should be completed.	Schedules are an extremely useful tool with children with autism. Since many children with autism respond well to visual cues, schedules and calendars provide useful support and prompting as well as promote self-management skills and independence.
SCRIPTING	Scripting occurs when an individual with autism is provided direction as to how to use language to initiate or respond in certain situations. A specific script is developed (verbal or written) which provides a model, and is practiced repeatedly before it is used in an actual situation.	Scripting is used alongside other behavioral interventions such as reinforcement, modeling, and promoting to help guide and teach the individual how to respond verbally to a situation. Scripts can be used in any setting and are a temporary teaching tool, designed to be faded out.
SELF-MANAGEMENT	Self-management techniques involve teaching individuals (typically adolescents between fourteen to twenty-one years) to evaluate and record their own performance while performing and completing a task or activity, to monitor social behaviors, to decrease and monitor disruptive behaviors, and to gain access to preferred activities when a task has been completed satisfactorily.	Self-management strategies are critical to learning and developing independence. As an individual learns to monitor their own behavior, they can work on increasing appropriate behaviors and decreasing maladaptive behaviors. This decreases their reliance on others and teaches critical skills for adulthood such as waiting for access to a preferred item or a reward (working and waiting for a paycheck).

INTERVENTION	DESCRIPTION	COMMENTS + EXAMPLES
SOCIAL SKILLS PACKAGE	The social skills package teaches the necessary skills to participate in social interactions at home, at school, and in community settings. The targeted skills are communication, play, and interpersonal skills. Programs can be one-on-one, in a peer or sibling dyad, or in a group setting.	Social skills are essential to success in all environments. The critical skills typically learned in early childhood such as joint attention, learning to share, taking turns, initiating an interaction, and solving problems are fundamental to lifelong independence and success.
STORY-BASED INTERVENTION	Story-based interventions identify a specific behavior and develop a story around that behavior to provide the individual with context, description, and perspective.	Social Stories™ are the most common form of this intervention. The stories help individuals with autism manage challenging situations and can be used in a wide variety of settings. For an example of a social story, please visit RonitMolko.com

INTERVENTION	DESCRIPTION	COMMENTS + EXAMPLES
EMERGING TREATMENTS: (Evidence is emerging to support these interventions—more studies are needed)		
AUGMENTATIVE AND ALTERNATIVE COMMUNICATION DEVICES	These interventions involve the use of technological devices (with varying levels of sophistication) to facilitate communication.	Examples of these systems are: picture communication systems, photographs, symbols, communication books, iPads, computers, mobile phones, and other electronic devices.
DEVELOPMENTAL RELATIONSHIP-BASED TREATMENT	Developmental relationship-based approaches are systematic approaches grounded in theories of human development and developmental pragmatics. These approaches build on the child's interests, occur in the natural environment, and focus on the interaction between the child and his environment over time. One approach, relationship development intervention (RDI) builds on the theory that dynamic intelligence/flexible thinking is key to improving quality of life for individuals with autism.	Research is limited and therefore these approaches are not considered established interventions. There is a lack of independent research to substantiate the efficacy of RDI. Despite this, parents do report that these approaches help their children develop dynamic intelligence and problem-solving approaches to life as well as relational skills that support better interpersonal relationships. Some consider these interventions unestablished and others consider them emerging interventions.

INTERVENTION	DESCRIPTION	COMMENTS + EXAMPLES
PICTURE EXCHANGE COMMUNICATION SYSTEM (PECS)	The picture exchange communication system, or PECS, allows people with little or no communication abilities to communicate using pictures. People using PECS are taught to approach another person and give them a picture of a desired item in exchange for that item. By doing so, the person is able to learn how to initiate communication and then start to develop more complex communication patterns.	Many people once opposed the use of PECS and sign language to teach children with autism to communicate out of fear that it would hurt the development of spoken language. Nowadays, there have been several studies that have shown PECS helps people develop verbal language. Language development can decrease tantrums and odd behaviors, and allows for increased socialization.
FUNCTIONAL COMMUNICATION TRAINING (FCT)	Functional communication training (FCT) is a procedure in which an individual is taught responses that are alternatives to a behavior that is maintaining a problem behavior.	By way of example, if a child is screaming to get attention, they are taught a communicative phrase or gesture as an alternative to screaming to get the same reinforcer: the attention.
SENSORY INTEGRATION THERAPY (SIT)	Based on the theory that autistic individuals have difficulty modulating sensory input and regulating emotion, learning, and behavior, SIT attempts to ameliorate processing difficulties through sensory integration. Treatments include using weighted vests and blankets, brushing, massages, fidget devices, therapy balls, and play activities to change how the brain reacts to touch, sound, sight, and movement.	Some parents and autistic individuals report anecdotally that SIT improves daily function, helps to calm them down and alleviates stress. While there is very limited research demonstrating efficacy, a recent study showed that children in the SIT group scored significantly higher on attaining their goals than children in the control group (Schaaf, 2014).
THEORY OF MIND TRAINING	These intervention are designed to teach individuals to recognize and identify mental states in themselves and others and to be able to take the perspective of another person in order to predict their actions.	One study has shown evidence for positive results, generalization, and maintenance of outcomes at twelve weeks after the conclusion of the intervention.

INTERVENTION	DESCRIPTION	COMMENTS + EXAMPLES
REDUCTIVE PACKAGE	This intervention uses strategies designed to reduce inappropriate behaviors in the absence of increasing alternative appropriate behaviors.	When measured, generalization has been demonstrated. One study showed maintenance of treatment gains for 12 months.
MUSIC THERAPY	This intervention teaches goals through music	One study showed that students generalized the skills learned during music therapy to a non-music therapy environment.
ADDITIONAL EMERGING EVIDENCE INTERVENTIONS: (please visit RonitMolko.com for more information)	Sign Instruction Social Communication Intervention Exercise Massage Therapy Multi-Component Package Imitation-Based Intervention	Technology-Based Intervention Structured Teaching Language Training (Production & Understanding) Initiation Training Exposure Package

INTERVENTION	DESCRIPTION	COMMENTS + EXAMPLES
UNESTABLISHED INTERVENTIONS: (Some of the most well-known controversial and alternative treatments without evidence to support efficacy)		
INTENSIVE VITAMIN THERAPIES	Up to 30 percent of families report using vitamin regimens which are extremely costly and can involve administering daily vitamin shots and upwards of thirty different vitamins per day.	While numerous studies have been conducted, most have flawed methodologies that make determinations about the efficacy of vitamin therapy inconclusive. In some studies there was no statistical difference between treatment and placebo groups, in another study, both groups showed a positive effect from the use of vitamins.
GLUTEN-FREE AND CASEIN-FREE DIETS	Dietary intervention by removing gluten and dairy based products entirely from the diet. Based on the theory of excess opioids in the system. Designed to alleviate symptoms of autism.	Reviews of studies show variable support for this theory. Studies have provided evidence against the opioid excess theory. Risks to the diet include decreased bone density and potential protein malnutrition. Currently, this diet is only recommended for children with a supported allergy to gluten and/or dairy or gut-related issues but is not recommended as an intervention for autism specifically.
SECRETIN (hormone that aids in digestion)	Targets gastrointestinal (GI) problems in children with autism (up to 50 percent of children with autism have GI issues).	A study describing three children with autism reported decreased GI discomfort and improved eye contact, alertness, and expressive language. This led to huge parental demand for this treatment. Follow-up double-blind placebo-controlled studies showed no evidence of a clinically significant effect from secretin as a treatment for autism.

INTERVENTION	DESCRIPTION	COMMENTS + EXAMPLES
CHELATION THERAPY	Based on the theory that autism is caused by exposure to toxins such as mercury poisoning, chelation therapy is designed to draw heavy metals out of the body via urination. This treatment is expensive. It is still featured on popular parents support group websites as a potential treatment.	Research has demonstrated no clear evidence of direct benefit from chelation therapy, and it can be very dangerous. The National Institute of Health cancelled a 2008 study due to health risks, and one family sued their doctor in 2010 for the death of their child from chelation therapy.
HYPERBARIC OXYGEN TREATMENT (HBOT)	HBOT is approved for illnesses such as decompression sickness, gas poisoning, burns, and involves inhaling oxygen in a pressurized chamber. HBOT has been used in autism to target oxidative stress, inflammation, and other brain functions (Rossignol, 2007) to target core behavioral symptoms in autism.	Follow-up studies have not shown a significant difference between treatment and control groups and HBOT has not been shown to be a clinically effective treatment for autism. The price for HBOT can cost more than $15,000 depending on the number of sessions provided.
ANIMAL THERAPIES	These therapies include service dogs, equestrian programs, and dolphin assisted therapy (DAT-swimming with dolphins). Dogs have been used as companions and for safety purposes (for children who may wander or run away) and behavioral improvement such as mood elevation, improved social skills, and increased attention have been reported.	Research regarding the effectiveness of animal-based therapies consists largely of individual case studies, parental reports, and anecdotal reports. There is little consistency regarding the mechanisms of action in these therapies reported in the research. It has been suggested that improvements in behaviors may be as a result of more frequent outings into the community (because the dog makes it more safe to do so), increased involvement in community activities, sensory calmness from horseback riding, and the connection between human and animal.

INTERVENTION	DESCRIPTION	COMMENTS + EXAMPLES
FACILITATED COMMUNICATION (FC)	FC is an augmented communication technique whereby individuals with limited communication skills can convey their thoughts by pointing to letters to spell out words or typing using a device. The user is supported by a trained facilitator who holds/guides/supports the individual's elbow, arm, or hand to assist them on pointing to, or typing out, letters. The intention is for the facilitator to support the individual's arm, hold it steady, not guide it, and fade their support over time so that the individual can communicate independently.	FC is controversial because of the inconsistency in ascertaining who has authored the message. Multiple research studies have demonstrated that facilitators have unknowingly influenced the written message and, as a result, multiple scientific and professional organizations have deemed the use of this procedure unethical. There have been multiple cases involving parents of children being falsely accused of sexual abuse and going to jail—allegations emerging via their FC communication. Please visit RonitMolko.com for more information.
AUDITORY INTEGRATION TRAINING (AIT)	Participants listen to sounds or music that are altered to affect the frequencies and volume. Benefits are purported to be improvements in eye contact, memory, articulation, social skills, and willingness to interact socially.	This treatment bases its utility on the notion that individuals with autism showing a higher incidence of sensory processing difficulties, one of which is difficulties processing and organizing auditory information. A review of the research shows that there was no significant difference between treatment and control groups, and no sufficient evidence to support the efficacy of this intervention. It is still considered an experimental treatment.
DIR/FLOORTIME	Based on the theory that autistic children experience biological differences that prevent typical interactions with caregivers and their environment, DIR is designed to encourage playful and positive interactions between child and caregiver to facilitate emotional and social growth.	Floortime is widely used in some areas and liked by some parents. There remains very little research to support this as an effective intervention for autism.

| MORE UNESTABLISHED INTERVENTIONS

(please visit RonitMolko.com for more information) | Concept Mapping
Movement-Based intervention
SENSE Theatre Intervention
Shock Therapy | Social Behavior Learning Strategy
Social Cognition Intervention
Social Thinking Intervention |

REFERENCES

"Findings and conclusions: National standards project, phase 2," National Autism Center, last modified 2015, http://www.nationalautismcenter.org/national-standards-project/phase-2.

Flippin M, Reszka S, Watson LR, "Effectiveness of the Picture Exchange Communication System (PECS) on communication and speech for children with autism spectrum disorders: a meta-analysis," Am J Speech Lang Pathol 19, no. 2 (May 2010): 178-95, doi: 10.1044/1058-0360(2010/09-0022).

Greenspan, Wieder, "DIR® / FloortimeTM Model," ICDL, last modified 2006, https://www.stanleygreenspan.com/suff The%20DIR%20Floortime%20Model.pdf.

Julie Young et al., "Autism Spectrum Disorders (ASDs) Services Final Report on Environmental Scan," IMPAQ International, last modified March 9, 2010, http://www.autismhandbook.org/images/8/8a/ASD_Services_Environmental_Scan.pdf.

Prizant, B., Wetherby, A., and Rydell, P., "Communication intervention issues for children with autism spectrum disorders," Autism spectrum disorders: A transactional developmental perspective 9, (2000).

"Resources," National Autism Resources, accessed March 30, 2018, www.nationalautismresources.com.

Rossignol, D. A., "Hyperbaric oxygen therapy might improve certain pathophysiological findings in autism," Medical Hypotheses 68, (2007): 1208–1227.

Schaaf, R.C., Benevides, T., Mailloux, Z. et al., "An Intervention for Sensory Difficulties in Children with Autism: A Randomized Trial," J Autism Dev Disord 44, no. 1493 (2014) 44: 1493, doi: /10.1007/s10803-013-1983-8.

Worley J., Fodstad J., and Neal D., (2014) Controversial Treatments for Autism Spectrum Disorders, In: Tarbox J., Dixon D., Sturmey P., Matson J. (eds) Handbook of Early Intervention for Autism Spectrum Disorders (Springer, New York, NY).

E mpowering Synergy is a team of corporate strategy consultants and due diligence consulting advisors dedicated to advancing outcomes for businesses and consumers of healthcare services with a specific focus and expertise in autism and developmental disorders.

After almost three decades as a service provider in the autism services industry, I was struck by the lingering insufficiencies in the quality of life and long-term outcomes for adults trying to work, live, and relate to others in our society. As the autism landscape changes and demands for outcomes shift, I recognized that increasing investor interest in this sector of the healthcare industry poses great potential for advancing how individuals with autism could function and live.

I founded my company, Empowering Synergy, to help investors and providers of behavioral healthcare services advance outcomes for autistic individuals, and other consumers of healthcare services, while building profitable and sustainable business models. The work we do is reflected in our values: knowing that individuals and organizations can be empowered to make positive, sustainable changes that improve their business, their lives, and the lives of those around them.

We quickly help investors understand the marketplace, the competitive landscape, as well as identify the strengths, differentiating factors, and risks in direct service companies to guide investment decisions and support ongoing growth and scale of investments. We help service providers expand their service models, develop strategic plans for growth and scale, manage regulatory environments, and prepare for investment opportunities.

I hope that this book has inspired you to look closely at how the services you provide and the investments you make will support individuals and families to achieve the lives they dream about. Empowering Synergy can guide your investment to make an impact, advance autism services, and improve lives.

To learn more about Empowering Synergy,
please visit **empoweringsynergy.com,**
email us at **connect@empoweringsynergy.com,**
or call **(424) 372-7996.**